Gardening in Dry Climates

Created and designed by
the editorial staff of
ORTHO BOOKS

Editor
Cedric Crocker

Writer
Scott Millard

Illustrator
Ron Hildebrand

Major Photographer
Saxon Holt

Designer
Gary Hespenheide

Ortho Books

Publisher
Robert J. Dolezal

Editorial Director
Christine Robertson

Production Director
Ernie S. Tasaki

Managing Editors
Michael D. Smith
Sally W. Smith

System Manager
Katherine Parker

National Sales Manager
Charles H. Aydelotte

Marketing Specialist
Dennis M. Castle

Operations Coordinator
Georgiann Wright

Distribution Specialist
Barbara F. Steadham

Administrative Assistant
Francine Lorentz-Olson

Senior Technical Analyst
J. A. Crozier, Jr., PhD.

Address all inquiries to
Ortho Books
Chevron Chemical Company
Consumer Products Division
Box 5047
San Ramon, CA 94583

Copyright © 1989
Chevron Chemical Company
All rights reserved under international and
Pan-American copyright conventions.

1 2 3 4 5 6 7 8 9
89 90 91 92 93 94

ISBN 0-89721-195-2
Library of Congress Catalog Card
Number 88-63839

Chevron Chemical Company
6001 Bollinger Canyon Road, San Ramon, CA 94583

Acknowledgments

Developmental Editor
Susan Lang

Copy Chief
Melinda E. Levine

Copyeditor
Frances Bowles

Layout Editor
Linda M. Bouchard

Systems Coordinator
Laurie Steele

Editorial Coordinator
Cass Dempsey

Proofreader
Deborah N. Bruner

Indexer
Frances Bowles

Editorial Assistants
Nicole Barrett
Karen K. Johnson
Tamara Mallory

Production by
Studio 165

Text separations by
Palace Press, Singapore

Cover separations by
Color Tech Corporation, U.S.A.

Lithographed by
Webcrafters, Inc., U.S.A.

Photo Editors
Lindsay Kefauver
Scott Millard

Additional Photographers
With the exception of the following, all photographs in this book are by Saxon Holt. Names of photographers are followed by the page numbers on which their work appears. R = right, C = center, L = left, T = top, B = bottom.

William Aplin: 78BR
Josephine Coatsworth: 6
John Harlow, Jr.: 13T, 26B
Eric Johnson: 8B, 12B
Michael Landis: 10T, 22T, 25T, 28B, 29T, 47, 54T
Michael MacCaskey: 100R
Michael McKinley: 74BL, 92TL
Charles Mann: 10B, 21T, 38, 62B, 63T, 73L, 73R, 79TR, 83R, 85L, 86R, 89R, 103BL, 103R, 104TR, 105
Scott Millard: 8T, 31, 34, 35T, 35C, 35B, 70, 71BR, 99R
Pam Peirce: 96L
Charles Sacamano: 26T, 55T, 56L, 56R, 79BR
Paul Serra: 24B
Daniel Snyder: 18B
Wolf von dem Bussche: 99L
Min Yee: 95TL
Ortho Photo Library: 65T, 65C, 65B, 71TL, 71TR, 71BL, 71C, 95R, 97R, 98

Special Thanks To
Eric Johnson, Palm Desert, Calif.
Susan Lang, Oakland, Calif.
Ron Lutsko, Jr., landscape architect, San Francisco, Calif.
Garden plan on page 27 based on design by Ron Lutsko, Jr.

Thanks To
Erika Aschmann, Water Conservation, EBMUD, Danville, Calif.
Joe and Allison Barta
Russell A. Beatty, University of California, Berkeley
Dick Bennett, Water Conservation, EBMUD, Danville, Calif.
The Blake Garden, Berkeley, Calif.
Botanical Garden, University of California, Berkeley
Shirley and Dave Bray, Albuquerque, N.Mex.
Tom Bressan, The Urban Farmer Store, San Francisco, Calif.
Gerald L. Chacon, Santa Fe, N.Mex.
Barrie D. Coate, Los Gatos, Calif.
Betty and Fred Crews
James K. Eggemeyer, landscape architect, Placerville, Calif.
Dr. and Mrs. Jay Feder, Albuquerque, N.Mex.
Jenny and Scott Flemming, Berkeley, Calif.
Dr. James R. Feucht, Colorado State University
Ron Gass, Mountain States Nursery, Phoenix, Ariz.
Alexandria Geremia, Santa Barbara, Calif.
Gail Haggard, Plants of the Southwest, Santa Fe, N.Mex.
M. Ali Haravandi, PhD., University of California Cooperative Extension, Alameda County
Dave Harbison, Coachella Valley Water District, Coachella, Calif.
Nancy Hardesty, Hardesty Associates, Menlo Park, Calif.
John Harlow, Jr., Harlow's Nursery, Tucson, Ariz.
J. Harris, Albuquerque, N.Mex.
Bill Hays, Albuquerque, N.Mex.
Richard Hine, PhD., University of Arizona, Tuscon
Warren D. Jones, University of Arizona, Tuscon
Charles Mann, Plants of the Southwest, Santa Fe, N.Mex.
Mudd's Restaurant, San Ramon, Calif.
Bill Nelson, Pacific Tree Farms, Chula Vista, Calif.
Emily Reed
Charles Sacamano, PhD., University of Arizona, Tuscon
SAWARA, Tucson, Ariz.
Paul Edward Serra, ASLA, WLB Group, Tucson, Ariz.
Jim Stalsonberg, San Deigo, Calif.
Ed Starkie, Hardesty Associates, Menlo Park, Calif.
Greg Starr, Starr Nursery, Tuscon, Ariz.
Strybing Arboretum, San Francisco, Calif.
Tohono Chul Park, Tucson, Ariz.
Marie Torrens, Albuquerque, N.Mex.
Catherine M. Trefethen
Tucson Botanical Gardens, Tucson, Ariz.
Michelle VanMeter, Tuscon, Ariz.
James Vlamis, PhD., Emeritus, University of California, Berkeley
Jim West, Soil and Plant Laboratory, Santa Clara, Calif.
Mr. and Mrs. Jerry Wilger, Albuquerque, N.Mex.
Carl Wilson, Colorado State University
Stuart Winchester, Diablo Valley College
Roger Wyer, Nature's Designs, Tucson, Ariz.

Front Cover
A northern New Mexico garden.

Title Page
A native plant and wildflower garden in Albuquerque, New Mexico.

Back Cover

Top left: Raised planting beds in an inland northern California garden.

Top right: Santa Barbara, Calif.

Bottom left: A drought-tolerant native and adapted plant landscape in coastal northern California.

Bottom right: Drip irrigation emitters deliver small, carefully controlled amounts of water.

Gardening in Dry Climates

Gardening in the Arid West

The arid West offers both challenges and rewards to the home gardener. An understanding of climate and soil conditions is an essential starting point for successful gardening.

What does it take to garden successfully in the arid West? It takes an understanding of western conditions—a western viewpoint. Western gardening practices are dictated by a particular set of climatic factors, including low rainfall, extremes of temperature, drying winds, and the problem soils that have resulted.

Gardeners accustomed to growing plants in the Midwest or East soon learn that many important rules change as they move westward. This change is especially true of the most precious resource in the arid West—water. Almost every gardener in the West faces the challenge of gardening in a hot, dry climate with a limited water supply that becomes more precious each year.

This book explains how to create a water-conserving garden, select the right plants, and provide the proper care so that the garden grows as envisioned.

First come the basics: a discussion of western climates—the general climate, the mesoclimates, and the microclimates—and their effect on gardening. Page 9 provides maps showing the arid West divided into 10 climate zones. With an awareness of climate firmly in mind, you will be well on your way to meeting the challenge of gardening in the West. The last chapter is devoted to plants and includes lists and charts of water-thrifty varieties to serve every function in the garden, as well as recommendations for planting edible crops.

This Santa Barbara garden displays the remarkable variety of color, texture, and form that can be achieved while still planting in harmony with the prevailing dry climate of the West.

THE WESTERN CLIMATES

The climate of the West is complex because of the effects of the Pacific Ocean and of coastal and inland mountain ranges. Along the coast, moisture and cool air from the ocean produce cool, foggy summers and mild, rainy winters. Inland, summers become hotter, winters colder, and rain is less likely to be confined to one season. The air grows colder as elevation increases.

The influence of the ocean lessens eastward until it is blocked by mountain ranges. Beyond are the deserts, formed as a result of blocked precipitation. The intense daytime heat of southwest deserts is caused by the southerly latitude of the region, the barrier provided by the Rocky Mountains against incoming arctic air, and the vast expanses of sand that absorb heat. Then, because there is normally no cloud cover to hold it in, this heat escapes after sunset, causing the typically chilly nights of the desert. At higher elevations in desert areas the weather is colder, day and night.

THE ELEMENTS OF THE ARID ENVIRONMENT

Several key elements—lack of rain, intense sun and heat, cold, wind, low humidity, and infertile soils—affect gardening in the arid West. To a large extent they determine gardening practices and should be kept in mind when establishing or tending a garden.

Rainfall

In the West, rainfall is meager, unpredictable, and unreliable. Except along the coast, the region receives little rainfall, as the climate charts on pages 106 to 107 demonstrate. Consider this sampling of annual rainfall statistics: Las Vegas, Nevada: 3.8 inches; Idaho Falls, Idaho: 8.9 inches; Phoenix, Arizona: 7 inches; Yuma, Arizona: 2.7 inches; Albuquerque, New Mexico: 7.8 inches; Palm Springs, California: 5.3 inches; San Diego, California: 9.4 inches. By comparison, most coastal cities of Oregon and Washington receive over 30 inches of rain per year.

When rain does fall in the West, its benefit is often limited. In some areas intense, localized summer storms dump large quantities of water in a very short time. For example, in Tucson, Arizona, almost 5 inches of the annual rainfall of 11 inches are received in July and August, delivered by tropical summer storms. Much of the rain falls in torrents, causing severe runoff and leaving little moisture to benefit plants.

In coastal California, as in other Mediterranean climates, nearly all rainfall occurs in winter. Under ideal conditions a series of moderate storms supplies the soil with enough moisture for deep-rooted plants to draw on throughout the year. During some years, however, there may be drought. In other years heavy downfalls may cause runoff or flooding.

Scrubby, low vegetation, hardy coniferous trees, and rocky, dry soil are common to many regions of the West, including this area around Santa Fe.

Sunlight and heat are a problem throughout the West. Adequate protection is essential.

Since rain cannot be relied upon to supply water for a garden throughout the year, gardeners must conserve the rain that does fall and make the best use of it. Suggestions for both may be found on pages 18 to 25 where low-water-use gardening is discussed, and on page 53, on the harvesting of water.

Sun and Heat

Too much sun and heat, especially when accompanied by a lack of water, can harm or even kill plants that are not adapted to the climate. This is particularly true of plants introduced from more temperate climates that have been placed in southern or western exposures, where sunlight and temperature are most intense.

At temperatures higher than 90° F, unadapted plants suffer because they are unable to transpire—use water evaporation to cool their tissues—quickly enough. Mature leaves dry out and turn brown around the edges, and leaf tips and new growth wilt. The soil temperature also increases, sometimes killing roots near the soil surface. Mulch—a thick layer of material over the plant roots—lowers the soil temperature and helps insulate the roots. See page 24 for information on mulching.

Even when temperatures are moderate, intense sunlight can burn unadapted plants. Yellowish white damage on older leaves is a sign of sunlight injury. Most damage occurs on bright, clear days. Sunlight reflected from light-colored walls or surfaces is even more intense. Under such conditions plant growth slows or stops. Ways of protecting plants from sun and heat are discussed on page 42.

Cold

Plant growth is affected by low temperatures as much as it is by high temperatures. When the temperature drops below a plant's low tolerance point, the tissues are damaged. The faster the temperature drops, the worse the injury. If the cold is severe or prolonged, the plant can die. In spring or early fall, when a plant is producing tender new growth, the damage caused by cold or frost is more severe than it would be if the new growth had hardened off—that is, adjusted gradually to cooler temperatures.

The most common frost is a radiational freeze, occurring during cool weather when humidity is low and there is no wind or cloud cover to keep warm air from escaping into the atmosphere. A more serious frost, although rare in most of the West, is the advective freeze or polar wave that occurs when a large cold air mass, usually from the north, moves into an area. It can cause major damage or death to plants that would survive normal low temperatures. Special care should be taken to protect valuable plants if a freeze is forecast. See Cold Protection, page 43.

Wind

Depending on its direction and velocity, and the season and temperature, the wind can be an advantage or a disadvantage. Wind of any kind, especially when accompanied by high temperatures, can dry out plants and increase their need for water. Plants that are not adapted to arid climates need to be watered more frequently during windy weather.

Many areas of the West experience damaging high winds, often in spring. In Las Vegas, for example, sandstorms with winds up to 40 miles per hour are common.

Gentle summer winds, because they have a cooling effect and make outdoor living more comfortable, should be encouraged. See page 30 for ideas on using plants to direct breezes.

Humidity

In much of the arid West, humidity is often 15 percent or less. Together with hot winds, high temperatures, and intense sunlight, such dryness can dehydrate plants quickly. Plants that are not adapted to dry weather can be damaged or killed in a short time unless they are watered adequately. Because the lack of humidity is difficult to counteract, choose suitable plants rather than trying to raise the humidity. Susceptible plants may be grouped close together to increase the relative humidity in a small area.

Soil

Western soils tend to be either sandy, holding little water, or claylike, holding little air. Organic matter improves both kinds of soils by restructuring them. In many parts of the United States where organic matter, such as decomposing leaves and stems, is plentiful, it works its way into the soil naturally. In much of the West, natural vegetation is sparse, and the decayed plant material that does end up in the soil dissipates quickly in hot weather. Consequently, it is important for western gardeners to amend the soil periodically or to use plants adapted to the native soil.

Other problems particular to soils of the arid West include alkalinity, salinity, and impenetrable layers such as caliche (a type of hardpan)—all of which can adversely affect plant growth. For more information on soils see the section beginning on page 34.

CLIMATE ZONES IN THE ARID WEST

In the West, climates range from the harsh winters of the Rocky Mountains and the Sierra Nevada, to the cool, moist, ocean-moderated conditions of the coast, and the severe heat of the deserts of the Southwest. This book concentrates on gardening in arid or dry regions, where moisture is scarce due to lack of rainfall, rapid evaporation, and low humidity.

Keep in mind that the figures listed here and in the rainfall and temperature charts on pages 106 and 107 are averages. Weather can change from year to year. Also the variable western terrain, which often changes mile by mile or from slope to valley to hilltop, can create different sets of weather conditions within the same general area. Read about mesoclimates and microclimates on page 14.

Top: Protection is needed against strong, sometimes unexpected, winds that can carry away soil and bring rapid changes in the weather.
Bottom: Western soils, as those in this California desert creek bed, are often rocky and poor in organic material.

Climate Zones of the Arid West

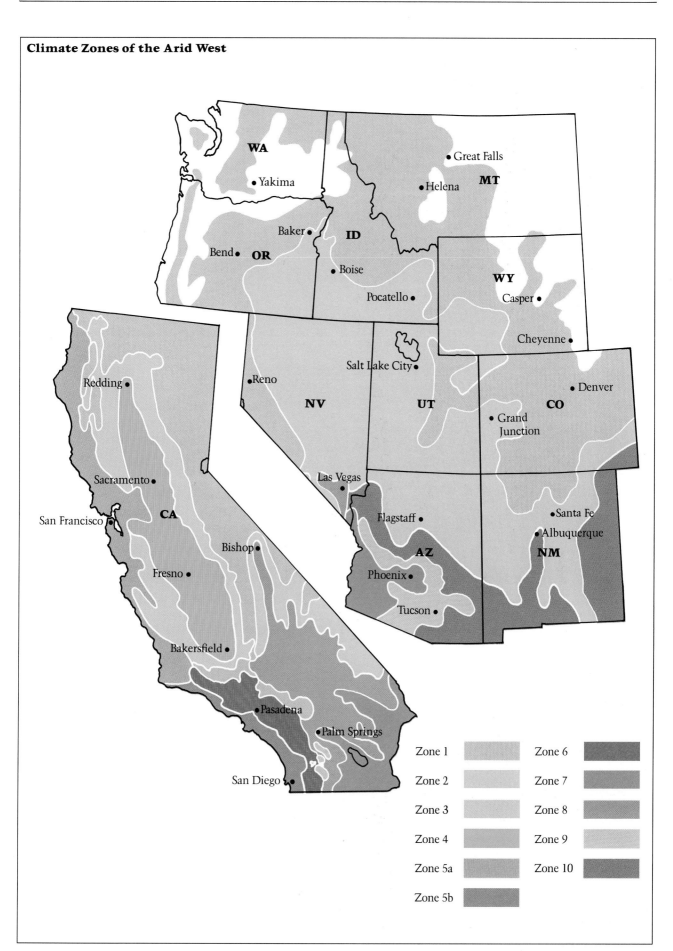

Zone 1
Zone 2
Zone 3
Zone 4
Zone 5a
Zone 5b
Zone 6
Zone 7
Zone 8
Zone 9
Zone 10

Zone 1: The Coldest Areas of the West

The coldest areas include the Rocky Mountains, the Sierra Nevada, the Cascades, and other regions of high elevation. Conditions in Reno, Nevada, and Cheyenne, Wyoming, are typical. Gardening here is unpredictable. Winter temperatures drop well below zero and the growing season usually lasts less than 150 days and sometimes (generally above 6,000 feet elevation) less than 100 days. Select plants for their tolerance to extreme cold. Conifers and cold-tolerant native plants are commonly used. Because of the short growing season, plant vegetable varieties that will reach maturity early. Cool-season crops are best. Grow annuals in containers so that they can be brought indoors when frost threatens.

Zone 2: The Great Basin and Eastern Colorado

Some of the coldest regions of the West are to be found in the Great Basin and in eastern Colorado. Milder climates prevail at lower elevations and close to rivers and other bodies of water. The growing season in this zone ranges from 100 to 150 days. The Great Salt Lake moderates temperatures around Salt Lake City, extending the growing season to 192 days. The Great Basin Desert, covering almost all of Nevada, extends up into southeastern Oregon and southern Idaho to include the cities of

Top: Despite very limited rainfall, high elevations, and a short growing season, this garden in Colorado supports an array of cosmos and zucchini plants, native conifers, and planted deciduous trees.
Bottom: Wildflowers and ground covers blend with the rugged native vegetation around this northern New Mexico home.

Boise, Twin Falls, and Pocatello. It also encompasses western and southeastern Utah and a portion of western Colorado. Average yearly rainfall in the Great Basin is 15 inches.

Native plants in the northern section of the Great Basin include sagebrush and bunchgrass. Woodland regions support Utah juniper and pinyon pine. In the mountains coniferous forests are common, as is snow. Temperatures at lower elevations, such as the Snake and Columbia river valleys and the plains regions, are more moderate, so less hardy plants can be grown successfully.

Soils are low in organic matter and often high in minerals. Gypsum added before planting will help modify the sodium content of alkali (sodic) soils. Soils around Salt Lake City are typically clay and drain slowly.

Zone 3: The Sierra Nevada Foothills and Coast Ranges of California

Also called the digger pine belt because the digger pine dominates the landscape, the Sierra Nevada foothills and Coast Ranges constitute a single climate zone. Various oaks, bay laurel, madrone, and California buckeye are native to this area. At one extreme, conditions and vegetation in the region are similar to those in the coldest regions of the West; at the other extreme, they are similar to conditions in warmer interior valleys. This is an area of distinct summers and winters, ideal for most deciduous fruits, such as peach and plum, that need marked seasonal changes. Rainfall is usually moderate but this region is subject to drought and occasional water rationing.

Zone 4: The Sacramento and San Joaquin Valleys

The climate zone of the Sacramento and San Joaquin Valleys stretches from Redding south through Sacramento, Davis, and Fresno to Bakersfield. The region, typical of California, has a variety of climatic conditions. Many thermal belts above valleys in the southern portion allow cold-tender plants, such as citrus, to thrive. Winter lows are moderate with averages in the mid-30° F range. A wide variety of plants can be grown. Crape myrtle, camphor, and pecan do well. High summer heat causes some trees, such as deodar cedar and Italian stone pine, to grow too rapidly, making

them short-lived and susceptible to insects and diseases. In the vegetable garden, melons thrive in the summer heat.

Zone 5: The California Coast and Coastal Valleys

Zone 5A, northern coast North of San Francisco the coast receives more rainfall than does the region south of the city, which itself gets 20 inches annually. Plants, particularly fruits, that require more extreme heat or cold, will not thrive in the moderate temperatures. Sweet citrus requires more heat, but sour citrus can be grown successfully. Many deciduous fruits need colder temperatures. This region is prime country for many California natives such as bay laurel and Monterey cypress. Hot weather and sporadic drought can occur on the coast and in nearby inland

Oak trees, hilly terrain, rocky soil, and dry summers make gardening in the California foothills a challenge. Hardy nandina has been planted on the upper slope and grevillea on the lower to add color to the garden.

valleys, and water is sometimes rationed. Soils vary greatly. In the San Francisco Bay Area there are sandy and clay soils as well as alkaline and acidic soils.

Zone 5B, southern coast The southern California coast and coastal valleys receive an average of less than 16 inches of rainfall annually (San Diego receives less than 10 inches a year), but the climate is not as arid as it is in California's inland valleys and deserts. High temperatures in summer are quite moderate. Many days are foggy. Humidity is much higher than it is in the inland areas, so plants simply do not need as much water. This is year-round gardening country and a haven for subtropical plants. The absence of summer heat prevents some heat lovers such as oleander and grapefruit from thriving. Deciduous fruits requiring cold also do poorly here.

Zone 6: The Interior Valleys of Southern California

The inland valleys of southern California in the vicinity of San Bernardino, Riverside, and Ontario are influenced much more by the warm interior deserts than by the Pacific Ocean. Summer temperatures often reach 100° F or more. In areas closer to Los Angeles—Pasadena, Glendale, and parts of the San Fernando Valley—ocean breezes moderate temperatures somewhat. For the most part this is prime citrus country. The growing season is long, stretching to 300 days or more for most of the region. Rolling, hilly terrain creates many small microclimates and low temperatures can be quite variable. Rainfall is moderate, averaging in the mid to high teens annually. Soils are variable, but tend to be sandy loam.

Zone 7: The Low Deserts of California and Arizona

This climate zone lies within the Sonoran Desert and includes Palm Springs and Indio in the Coachella Valley, as well as Blythe and El Centro, and extends as far east as Phoenix, Arizona. Summers are very hot, with highs often over 110° F. The growing season is long, stretching to 334 days in Palm Springs. Differences in soils and summer temperature extremes greatly affect plant selection and gardening practices. Soils in the Coachella

Top: The intermediate desert of Arizona. Bottom: The high desert of New Mexico. Opposite top: Raised beds make efficient use of water in this coastal northern California garden. Opposite center: Santa Barbara provides ideal conditions for many subtropical plants. Opposite bottom: Parts of the California low desert receive less than 6 inches of rain each year.

fornia and Nevada. The climate is similar to that of the intermediate desert of Arizona, but variations are much more extreme. Summer days are hot, 100° F or more, and are followed by cold nights. Winter lows are more drastic, often dropping below zero. Unless planted in a sheltered location, cold-tender plants such as citrus cannot be grown. Strong winds through the spring months are common, and homes and plants greatly benefit from windbreaks and shelterbelts.

Zone 9: The Intermediate Deserts of Arizona

Elevations in the intermediate deserts of Arizona average between 2,000 and 2,500 feet, resulting in winter temperatures cold enough to preclude subtropical plants or at least to require use of sheltered microclimates. In Tucson and other cities in southern Arizona rain relieves the summer heat during most years. Tucson normally receives 2 to 3 inches more rain in July and August than does Phoenix, 100 miles north. Soils are either heavy clay or very sandy, and are usually alkaline, with a pH of 7.5 or higher. It is not cold enough to grow deciduous fruit trees with high chilling requirements.

Zone 10: The High Deserts of Arizona and New Mexico

Zone 10 is represented by high deserts in the vicinity of the cities of Albuquerque, Deming, and Roswell, in New Mexico, and Kingman, Bisbee, Douglas, Globe, and Sedona, in Arizona. High temperatures are lower than those of the low and intermediate deserts of Arizona and California. Winter temperatures drop to 8° F. As a rule the temperature drops 5° F for each 1,000-foot rise in elevation.

Santa Fe typically has winter lows 8° F cooler than the rest of the climate zone, with a growing season of 178 days compared with an average for the climate zone of 191 days. In eastern New Mexico daily, monthly, and annual temperatures fluctuate widely. Snow falls throughout the zone, with as little as 2 to 5 inches a year in the lower Rio Grande Valley and almost 300 inches a year on the main ridge of the Sangre de Cristo Mountains. Soils of this region are alkaline and low in organic matter. Hard soils may benefit from the addition of large quantities of gypsum.

Valley tend to be light, sandy, and fast-draining, making frequent irrigation necessary. Soils in Phoenix are claylike and drain slowly, and are both alkaline and saline. The average July maximum of 110° F in Palm Springs compares with 105° F in Phoenix. Winds, usually sweeping in from the west, are very common from March through June in the Coachella Valley. Protect plants and water daily during these periods.

Zone 8: The Intermediate and High Deserts of California and Nevada

Lancaster, Palmdale, Barstow, Victorville, and Las Vegas are all situated in the climate zone of the intermediate and high deserts of Cali-

MESOCLIMATES: THE INTERMEDIATE CLIMATES

The 10 zones described in this chapter indicate the general range of climate in the arid West. Mountain ranges and large bodies of water will affect the climate of their immediate vicinity, creating what is known as a mesoclimate that may differ significantly from the general climate of the zone. San Diego, California, for example, enjoys its own mesoclimate. The coastal area is often shrouded by cooling fog during summer, while less than 20 miles inland, El Cajon has temperatures 30 to 40° F higher because of its proximity to desert.

MICROCLIMATES: THE SMALL-SCALE CLIMATES

Climate can change from street to street, from the bottom of a slope to the top, or even from one side of a house to the other. Structures, plants, and differences in elevation combine to create microclimates, climates-within-climates. There can be many microclimates within a single garden. For example, a cool, shady microclimate may be found on the north side of a house, a hot one in an unprotected southwestern corner, a cold one in a hollow at the bottom of a hill, a humid one near a dense planting of shrubs, and so on.

Microclimates

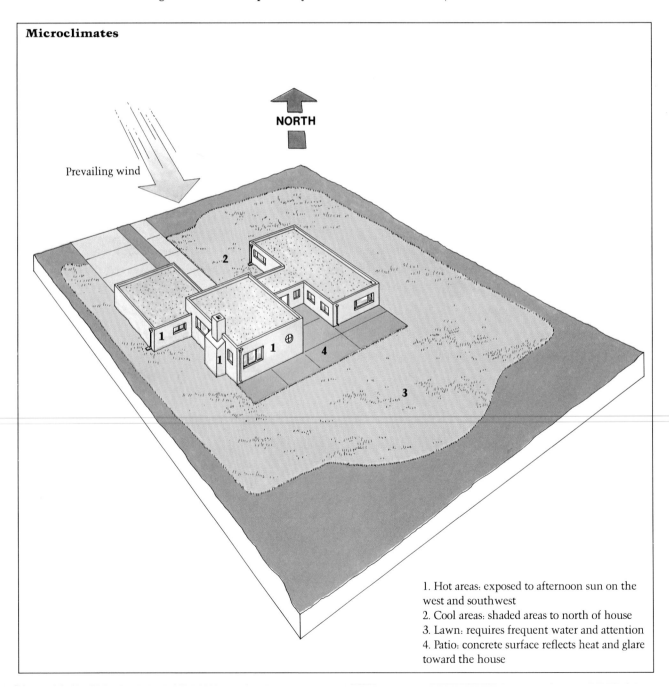

NORTH

Prevailing wind

1. Hot areas: exposed to afternoon sun on the west and southwest
2. Cool areas: shaded areas to north of house
3. Lawn: requires frequent water and attention
4. Patio: concrete surface reflects heat and glare toward the house

Take advantage of your microclimates. Plant cold-hardy, shade-loving plants on the north side of the house. Select heat-tolerant plants for a southwestern exposure. You may find, for example, a microclimate hot enough for a lemon tree, even if the region is not generally favorable for citrus.

Microclimates change with time. On a new homesite, the only shade may occur beneath overhangs, under the patio roof, and in the northern exposure. As plants grow, the amount of shade, temperatures, wind patterns, humidity, and other elements that make up microclimates also change. By learning to adapt to these changes, you can create a garden that transcends the general climate and takes advantage of your own property.

Top: This ridge of mountains in northern New Mexico creates a distinct mesoclimate. Center: To create a woodland of native plants, the owners of a northern California home have taken advantage of the shady, moist microclimate created by cool air flowing down the slope.

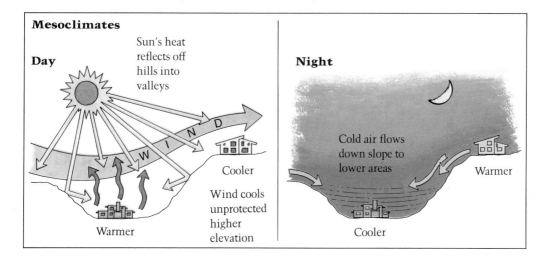

Mesoclimates

Day

Sun's heat reflects off hills into valleys

WIND

Cooler

Wind cools unprotected higher elevation

Warmer

Night

Cold air flows down slope to lower areas

Warmer

Cooler

Living in the Arid Environment

By designing or adapting your garden to make the most of the climate and scarce water, living in the arid environment can be comfortable and rewarding.

Two important aspects of gardening in the arid, often inhospitable environment of the West are discussed in this chapter: creating a water-conserving garden and modifying the climate around your home. Water is at a premium in the arid West, and water conservation is almost always necessary. The following pages explain the principles of low-water-use gardening and show how to arrange a garden according to those principles. This chapter contains guidance in grouping plants by their water need and using drought-tolerant plantings in place of high-water-use plantings. Other features of low-use, such as mulching and maintaining the garden, are discussed. Ideas for lawn alternatives are given. For a gardener who wants a lawn, there is advice on how to reduce its size and where to place it. Although most of the plants in a water-conserving garden use little water, there is provision for a small high-water-use area—a small oasis in which gardeners can indulge their interest in plants that require more moisture.

This chapter also explains how to modify sun, heat, and wind to create a more pleasant environment. Plants or structures can be used for this purpose. For example, deciduous trees or vines positioned carefully will create cooling shade in the summer and allow sunny warmth to filter through in the winter. There is also advice on controlling wind and reducing fire danger.

Although it may not look arid, this coastal northern California garden receives less than 20 inches of rain annually. Drought-tolerant native and adapted plants—such as the evergreen coast live oak—provide a variety of colors and textures throughout the year.

CREATING A WATER-CONSERVING GARDEN

A water-conserving garden may also be called a drought tolerant or low-water-use landscape, or a xeriscape (from the Greek word *xeros*, meaning *dry*). It is sometimes described as a zoned or natural garden. These terms generally refer to the same thing: a garden that is visually pleasing as well as practical, consists of native or adapted plants, and is one in which water is used efficiently.

The techniques of xeriscape described here are based on guidelines from the National Xeriscape Council. They can be used in a new garden or to modify a water-wasting garden. A xeriscape doesn't mean giving up anything—there are only gains: reduced water use, healthier plants, shortened maintenance time, and a deeper appreciation of the environment.

PRINCIPLES OF XERISCAPE

- ☐ Group plants with similar water needs
- ☐ Use drought-tolerant plants
- ☐ Limit lawn area
- ☐ Replace high-water-use plants
- ☐ Irrigate efficiently
- ☐ Improve the soil
- ☐ Use mulch
- ☐ Keep up with maintenance

Group Plants With Similar Water Needs

By grouping plants according to water need gardeners are able to concentrate moisture where it will do the most good instead of spreading it over the entire garden. Grouping or zoning plants allows you to create a visually interesting garden that is easier and less expensive to irrigate and maintain.

Zoning helps ensure that plants get the amount of water they need. Plants placed

Top: Place water-demanding plants closest to the house; there they will be most visible and appreciated. The lushness of this Albuquerque lawn creates an oasis and serves as a transition to the drier planting zones beyond. Bottom: Low-maintenance native plants and river rock have been used to transform a backyard near Tucson into an inviting oasis.

without regard for their water needs are usually given water whether they need it or not. Too much water can kill drought-tolerant plants, just as not enough can kill thirsty plants. Even thirsty plants given excess water can suffocate or become susceptible to diseases.

Three basic water-use zones are recommended for a xeriscape: low, moderate, and high. You may choose to limit yourself to low-water-use plants or a combination of low- and moderate-water-use plants. Don't feel that you should forgo a high-water-use zone because it seems wasteful. If confined to a small area, such a zone is perfectly acceptable as part of a water-conserving garden.

Low-water-use zone   Established plants in a low-water-use zone can thrive on annual rainfall alone, although some may require a deep soaking once or twice during the growing season to look their best. This area should be situated farthest from the house. Plants at the outer edges of the property need not be as lush, since they are usually viewed from a distance.

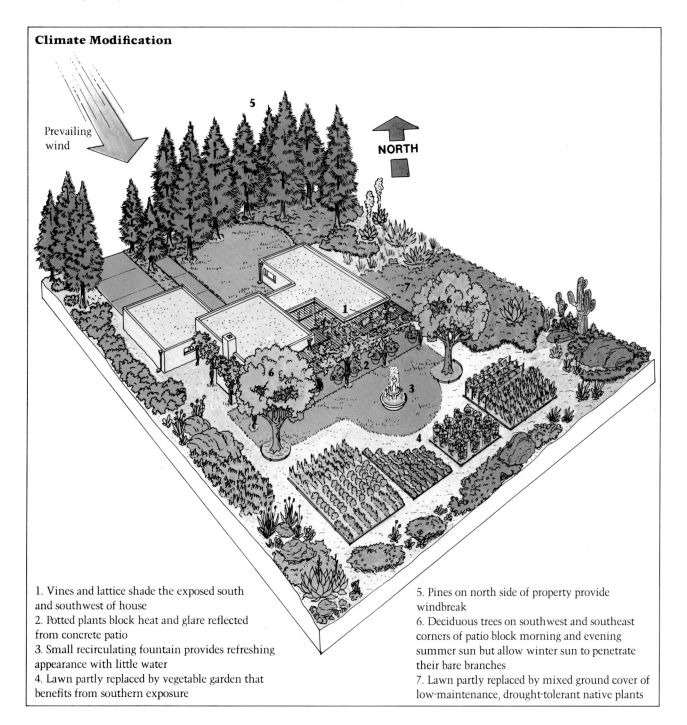

Climate Modification

Prevailing wind

NORTH

1. Vines and lattice shade the exposed south and southwest of house
2. Potted plants block heat and glare reflected from concrete patio
3. Small recirculating fountain provides refreshing appearance with little water
4. Lawn partly replaced by vegetable garden that benefits from southern exposure
5. Pines on north side of property provide windbreak
6. Deciduous trees on southwest and southeast corners of patio block morning and evening summer sun but allow winter sun to penetrate their bare branches
7. Lawn partly replaced by mixed ground cover of low-maintenance, drought-tolerant native plants

However, lushness and high water use don't always go hand in hand: some low-water-using plants look as good close up as their thirsty counterparts.

Moderate-water-use zone Plants for a moderate-water-use zone require some continuing irrigation, but not much—irrigation every couple of weeks or a deep soaking once a month during the growing season. They can serve as a transition between natural-looking plants at the outer edges of the yard and more lush plants near the house.

High-water-use zone Like an oasis in the desert, a high-water-use zone in a xeriscape can be a focal point in the garden or create a sense of coolness that contrasts with the surrounding landscape. In a small, lush area thirsty plants are grouped for maximum visibility and pleasure. Expend your water budget in the way you will appreciate it most: perhaps on a vegetable garden near the kitchen, on containers of dwarf citrus trees for the patio, or on a small patch of lawn.

Use Drought-Tolerant Plants

Plants that require little or no water after they are established are available to perform every function in the garden, including providing spectacular color. It is a matter of identifying the job you want plants to do and then selecting adapted water-thrifty plants to accomplish the task. The lists beginning on page 66 and the plant charts beginning on page 72 offer specific suggestions for such plants.

Even drought-tolerant plants will not always survive on their own from the start. It takes at least one or two full seasons of regular watering before plants are established and able to tolerate drought.

Degrees of drought tolerance Match plants with the conditions that make them drought tolerant. For example, some plants will only tolerate drought when growing in shade. In full sun they will need more moisture. Such requirements are noted in the culture column of the plant lists.

There is a difference between plants that can survive on little or no water after being established and plants that will thrive under those conditions. The latter will put on a good

Opposite: Group plants according to their water needs. Here, low-water-use grevillea and juniper surround the lawn. Right: Thick, glossy leaves are characteristic of many drought-tolerant plants, such as this manzanita.

Opposite: Two varieties of sage plants bracket groundsel (center), a relative of dusty-miller. Despite differences in appearance, all three plants require about the same amount of moisture to thrive.

Opposite: Many drought-tolerant plants are colorful. Blue and red penstemon blend with a ground cover of thyme and a lawn in this New Mexico garden.

species) have sticky leaves. Some, such as agave, have fat succulent leaves that store water. Small-leaved plants—for example, thyme, lavender, and artemisia—tolerate drought because the leaf surface is reduced. To cut down on water loss, many desert plants, such as cactus, have leaves reduced to spines or no leaves at all. Other plants have hairy surfaces that hold water. Gray or silver foliage, such as that of lamb's-ears (*Stachys byzantina*), is covered with fine hairs that insulate the leaves below.

Limit Lawn Area

Most lawns require a lot of water to look their best. The shallow root system of conventional lawn grasses dries out rapidly, particularly in sandy, fast-draining soil. In many areas lawns account for over half of a household's water use. Of necessity, attitudes toward the desirability of a large expanse of lawn in the arid West are changing as more people realize that water is limited.

If you feel you cannot eliminate the lawn, at least reduce it to a size that is just large enough to satisfy your needs. Almost always, it is more practical to treat a lawn as a functional ground cover rather than as an aesthetic feature. With its tight-knit strength and resilience, a lawn is an excellent surface for foot traffic and play. It should be placed where members of the household spend most of their time outdoors—usually in the backyard. If possible, locate it close to the house as part of a high-water-use zone.

show day after day with little or no supplemental irrigation; the former may not die but may not look very healthy either. Such plants are probably best when grown at the outer edges of the garden where they are less visible or when given the occasional deep soaking.

Recognizing drought-tolerant plants All drought-tolerant plants have a number of recognizable characteristics of their adaptation to dry climates. Plants with underground storage organs, such as bulbs and rhizomes, can usually tolerate drought. Other plants may show drought tolerance in the kinds of leaves they have. To hold moisture, some plants such as carob (*Ceratonia siliqua*) have thick waxy leaves, and some such as rockrose (*Cistus*

A limited lawn area near the house, colorful but low-water-use plants, mulch, and a carefully planned drip watering system make this San Diego garden a successful xeriscape.

To conserve water, don't plant a lawn on a slope of more than 6 percent. Keep the shape simple and easy to water.

Because a lawn needs to be watered frequently, don't mix it with other plants that are unaccustomed to so much moisture. Trees planted in lawns become shallow rooted and just as thirsty as the lawn. Studies also suggest that lawn grasses produce chemical inhibitors that slow the growth of competing plants.

Drought-tolerant lawn grasses If your lawn grass needs a lot of water, consider replacing it with a drought-tolerant species. There are two categories of grasses: cool-season grasses, which grow better in cool climates and remain green the year around if temperatures remain above freezing, and warm-season grasses, which grow better in warmer climates and become dormant when temperatures drop below 55° F to 60° F. Cool-season grasses require more water than do warm-season grasses.

Tall fescue (*Festuca elatior*) is the most drought tolerant of the cool-season grasses. It does need more water than zoysiagrass, the most drought tolerant of the conventional warm season lawn grasses. Zoysiagrass (*Zoysia matrella*) is widely adapted in southern climates except at high elevations where it snows. 'El Toro' is a particularly good variety.

Bermudagrass (*Cynodon dactylon*), another warm-season grass, also needs more water than does zoysiagrass but is still quite drought tolerant. Common bermudagrass is more tolerant than are the improved varieties.

Native grasses Some native grasses can be used as lawns. They aren't as lush and don't work as well for play surfaces as do conventional lawn grasses, but they make up for that with their adaptability to little water and adverse conditions. Mowing is required just three or four times a season.

Buffalograss (*Buchloe dactyloides*), a warm-season grass, is the most useful and most widely adapted of the native grasses. It grows just as well in the desert heat as in the cooler climate of the San Francisco Bay Area. Buffalograss seed is available and sod is being developed. Blue grama (*Bouteloua gracilis*), a warm-season native grass resembling buffalograss, is not as available or as widely adapted.

Lawn alternatives Lawn substitutes that accept foot traffic—for example, lippia (*Phyla nodiflora*) or dichondra (*Dichondra micrantha*)—often grow better in cooler, moist coastal areas. In hotter regions they generally need regular water to look their best.

The lawn can be replaced entirely. A deck or patio will provide recreation space. Many drought-tolerant plants, including manzanita (*Arctostaphylos*), ceanothus, creeping St.-Johnswort (*Hypericum calycinum*), or woolly yarrow (*Achillea tomentosa*) will provide a green ground cover.

Also possible is a mixed planting set among natural-looking contours and mounds or along a creek bed. Such plantings are easy to create and serve two purposes: they're interesting to look at and during the rainy season the creek can be used to channel water to storage containers. Add a few boulders to the area and then plant colorful, water-efficient shrubs, ground covers, and a few accent plants for more color.

Replace High-Water-Use Plants

Reduce water consumption by replacing plants that need plenty of water with drought-tolerant species. This can be done all at once, but will be easier if done gradually.

Replacing small plants is usually no problem, but think twice about removing mature specimens. Don't eliminate a healthy, fully grown tree simply because it requires water. If it is deep rooted, it may not need as much

Opposite: Thirsty Kentucky bluegrass has been replaced with Bermudagrass surrounded by mondograss.

Opposite: Natives such as buffalograss make a handsome lawn and require less frequent watering and cutting than nonnative varieties.

Opposite: Substitute low ground covers such as manzanita in areas where a lawn is not needed.

Where a lawn would serve only an aesthetic purpose, consider plants, such as this yellow-flowering cinquefoil, which create a pleasing and practical ground cover. Saltbush (center right) is used as an accent in a New Mexico garden.

The bright colors of a perennial garden are created with low-water-use plants—agapanthus, oleander, sage, marguerites, and others—in front of this San Diego home.

water as you're giving it. Also consider the fact that mature, healthy plants may add value to your home. Consult a licensed professional if you're not sure whether replacement is the right answer.

Plan the conversion carefully, first evaluating your garden for its water needs and determining which plants you want to replace. To keep your garden attractive while it is being converted and spread the time, effort, and expense over a longer period, replace plants in stages. Dispose of the largest and thirstiest plants first.

Irrigate Efficiently

With efficient irrigation, plants are given only as much water as they need, when they need it. There is little or no waste. It depends first on grouping plants with similar water needs and then using an irrigation system that accomplishes the objective.

Drip or low-volume irrigation is the most practical system, for all plantings except lawns in the arid West. It directs water precisely where it's needed and only as fast as the soil can absorb it. For more information on drip systems, see page 56.

A lawn is best watered by overhead sprinklers. Because it needs more water than other plantings, it should be irrigated separately and the system should have its own control valve or timer. See Watering a Lawn, page 52.

Improve the Soil

Organic matter, such as decomposed bark or leaves, added to sandy soils increases their ability to hold water and nutrients so that plants don't have to be irrigated or fed as often. Although clay soils hold water and nutrients well, they have inadequate air space and plants can suffocate when the soil is saturated. Organic matter improves aeration in clay soils and allows water to be absorbed more easily so that there is less runoff during rainstorms. For more information on soils, see the section beginning on page 34.

Use Mulch

Mulch—any material that covers the soil—has several important roles in a low-water-use garden: it conserves moisture in the soil, moderates the soil temperature, and suppresses weeds that compete with plants for moisture.

Organic mulches gradually work their way downward and improve the soil. Mulching also reduces soil erosion and protects the soil from being compacted by foot traffic or heavy rains.

A mulch of medium-sized particles is usually best. Small-particle mulches can be blown or washed away and large particles tend to leave unprotected gaps. Fine mulches can also become compacted, inhibiting water penetration and aeration of the soil. To be effective, a mulch should be applied in a 3- to 4-inch layer. Be sure to keep it away from plant stems or trunks, where it can cause rot. Some native plants are particularly sensitive to rot and fare better with an inorganic mulch of loose stones or gravel that won't become compacted. A local native plant society can offer advice on the best mulch material for specific plants.

Keep Up With Maintenance

Even a simple garden needs a certain amount of upkeep. Plants that are properly maintained grow better, are more attractive, and require less care in the long run. It is important to inspect plantings, particularly new ones, regularly to be sure they are in good shape.

See the sections on weeding and pruning on pages 40 to 42 and protecting plants beginning on page 42.

*Top: Mulch can serve as an attractive ground cover.
Bottom: Regular maintenance is essential to keeping a xeriscape attractive.
Opposite top: Drip irrigation is the most efficient—and least visible—method for watering individual plants. Note the drip tubing and emitter.
Opposite center: Mulch insulates plant roots and retains moisture in the soil.
Opposite bottom: A variety of gravel and rock reduces maintenance and water use in this garden in southern Arizona.*

LIVING COMFORTABLY IN THE ARID WEST

Climate—including mesoclimates and micro-climates—greatly affects living and gardening in the West. In hot, arid areas climatic forces can create unpleasant living conditions. Plants and structures may be used to modify heat, cold, and wind.

Modifying Sunshine and Heat

Plants help control summer sun and heat by shading structures and outdoor living areas, insulating exterior walls, and reducing reflected light and glare.

Trees for shade   Trees create cooling shade outdoors as well as reduce energy costs for cooling the home's interior. The University of Arizona Cooperative Extension Service reports that exterior shading is seven times more effective than is interior cooling. A tree with a dense canopy of leaves can screen out 80 percent of the sun's radiation, reducing a home's interior temperature by up to 20 percent. See illustration, page 27.

In the West, the sun appears high in the sky but never directly overhead, so a tree is never able to cast all of its shade beneath itself. Because of the angle of the sun, trees and other objects cast short shadows that lengthen as the season changes.

A shade tree should be positioned to block the hot summer sun, and is best placed to the southeast or southwest of a building or patio. Because of the path of the summer sun, a tree

Summer Shade/Winter Sun

Summer   Winter

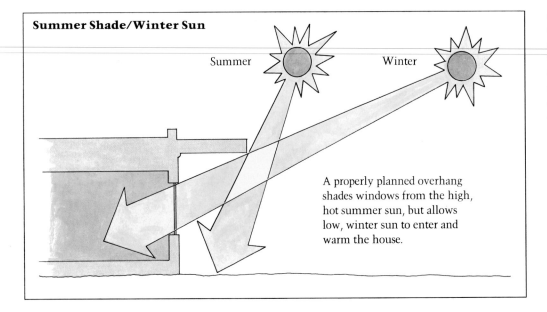

A properly planned overhang shades windows from the high, hot summer sun, but allows low, winter sun to enter and warm the house.

Place deciduous trees on the south side of a building where they will provide shade in the summer and allow the warm winter sun to penetrate their leafless branches.

Summer Shade   ### Winter Sun

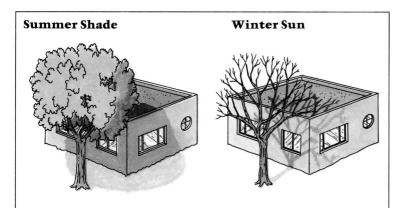

Place deciduous trees on the southeast and southwest of the house to provide shade in summer and—when the leaves fall—allow winter sun to penetrate.

on the south side of a house is not able to cast its shadow on the structure, unless it is very tall and planted close to the building. See the illustrations, at left and below.

Beneficial winter sun   The winter sun warms the house and lowers energy bills, particularly in cold high-desert areas and in and around the Great Basin.

Deciduous trees, such as honey locust (*Gleditsia triacanthos*), Osage-orange (*Maclura pomifera*), or certain species of mesquite (*Prosopis*) will give you the best of both worlds—summer shade and winter sun.

Water Conserving Garden

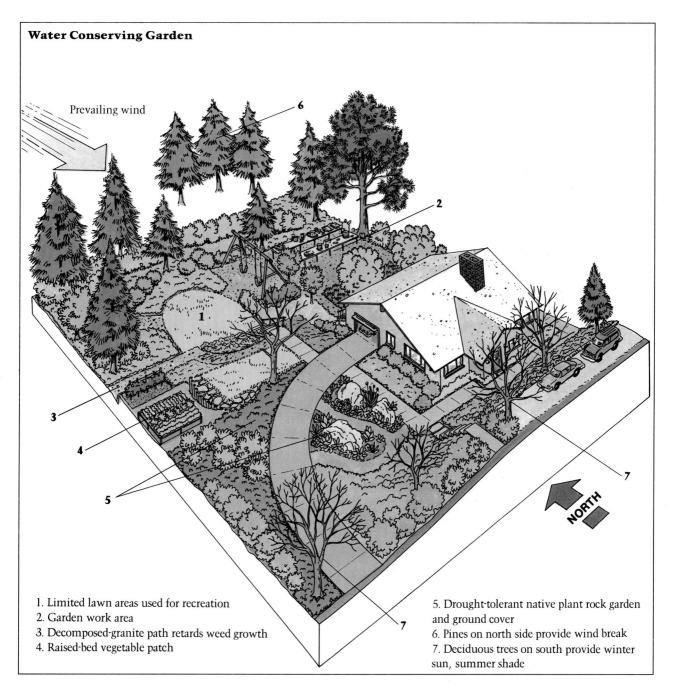

Prevailing wind

1. Limited lawn areas used for recreation
2. Garden work area
3. Decomposed-granite path retards weed growth
4. Raised-bed vegetable patch

5. Drought-tolerant native plant rock garden and ground cover
6. Pines on north side provide wind break
7. Deciduous trees on south provide winter sun, summer shade

The intense summer sun is blocked by a screen of woven wood. The screen may be removed in winter to admit warming winter sun.

The combination of a lattice and vine is one of the many different forms of screening that may be used to shade south-, east-, and west-facing windows.

onto their leaves or others such as catalpa, which bear large seed pods late into the season, also block winter sun.

Evergreen trees should not be planted near the house or patio on the east, south, and southwest exposures if winter sun is desired.

Vines for shade   Climbing plants do an excellent job of creating summer shade and controlling heat—and they produce it faster than young trees are able to. Supported by a trellis or other structure, a fast-growing vine makes an effective sun screen quickly. Plant a deciduous vine if you want shade in summer and sun in winter. A grapevine will grow quickly to cover arbors and trellises with greenery that is shade producing, then drop its leaves in winter to allow the warming sun to shine through.

Structures for shade   Latticework, usually sold in 4- by 8-foot panels, is an inexpensive shade producer. Available at most home building centers, it can be used alone for immediate shade or as a support for vines. Used alone, latticework can be covered with shade cloth, which is available in different densities (measured in percentages) that limit the amount of sunlight that comes through. The cloth can be rolled back during winter to allow as much sun through as possible.

Because deciduous trees lose their leaves in winter, the warm winter sun can shine through the branches to reach the house or patio. Choose a tree with an open branching habit. The silk tree (*Albizia julibrissin*) and many species of alder (*Alnus*) are among trees that can block winter sun because of their branching habits. Trees such as sweet gum (*Liquidambar styraciflua*) that hold

An espaliered blue atlas cedar has been used to shade and insulate the south side of this house.

Reducing reflected heat and glare   Paved areas, gravel, and masonry walls store heat and radiate it back after sundown. Test this by feeling the warmth emanating from a south- or west-facing wall after the sun has set. This increase in outside temperature can increase the indoor temperature, making you turn up the air conditioner a notch. Reduce the heat by using plants that grow vertically or train plants as espaliers. Espaliers insulate wall surfaces by providing dead air space and they cool temperatures by evapotranspiration—a term used to describe the moisture that evaporates from the soil together with the water that the plant transpires to cool itself. In frost-free areas bougainvillea is a favorite vine to train against a wall. In colder regions try yew pine (*Podocarpus macrophyllus*) or an upright juniper. Keep plants at least 6 inches away from walls or the foliage may burn.

Paved areas, particularly light-colored ones, reflect sunlight, as does water from a swimming pool. Homes with swimming pools or large paved areas in west-facing backyards provide perfect conditions for annoying glare. Intense bright light from a setting summer sun can be reflected into the interior of a home and will make outdoor patios unbearable during the late afternoon.

Reducing Reflected Heat and Glare

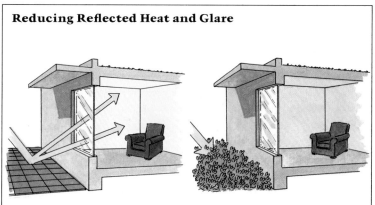

Overhangs eliminate only some sunlight. Cover concrete surfaces beneath windows with potted plants, or replace those surfaces entirely with a drought-tolerant ground cover.

Ground-cover plants placed around the paving or pool will diffuse the sunlight. In mild-winter areas use tough, heat-tolerant varieties such as manzanita (*Arctostaphylos*) and rosemary (*Rosmarinus*); in cold-winter regions, a low-growing juniper or cotoneaster.

Modifying Wind

Before attempting to control wind, observe the seasonal wind patterns and note the prevailing directions. Winds generally come from the north in winter and the south in summer. Along the Pacific coast, winds tend to be westerly. One way to tell wind direction in your

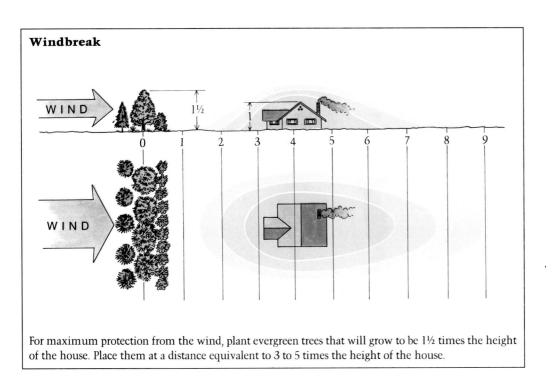

Windbreak

WIND

1½

0   1   2   3   4   5   6   7   8   9

WIND

For maximum protection from the wind, plant evergreen trees that will grow to be 1½ times the height of the house. Place them at a distance equivalent to 3 to 5 times the height of the house.

Top: Trees and walls shield the garden from the heavy, constant winds of the plain beyond, and provide privacy and visual appeal.
Bottom: A line of Russian-olive trees breaks the wind.

garden or neighborhood is to note the way in which trees lean.

Windbreak   A windbreak is any barrier that slows or dissipates the flow of wind. It should be placed between the wind and the house. Construct a windbreak to allow some wind to pass through; otherwise, when the wind passes over the windbreak, it comes down with greater force creating turbulence directly behind the barrier.

Plant dense evergreen trees or shrubs that will grow to one and a half times the height of the house. Planted at a distance equaling three to five times the height of the house, the trees will lift most winds over the house and outdoor areas. A windbreak planted at a distance equal to twice the height of the house may be useful in areas, such as Las Vegas, where extreme winds are common.

Before planting the windbreak, consider the shading effect that evergreens may have on the house. You will have to balance the benefits of a windbreak with the decreased exposure to winter sun.

Plants that work well as windbreaks include pine, cypress, pittosporum, California pepper (*Schinus molle*), coast live oak (*Quercus agrifolia*), and evergreen species of elaeagnus. See additional suggestions on page 66. Do not plant pines or other flammable trees close to a house in areas where fires are likely.

Directing Wind

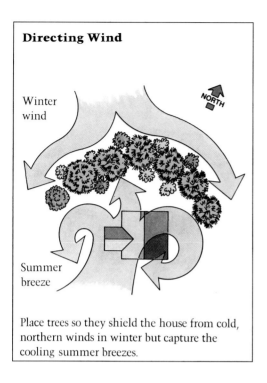

Winter wind

NORTH

Summer breeze

Place trees so they shield the house from cold, northern winds in winter but capture the cooling summer breezes.

Large, open properties may require a shelterbelt planting of evergreen trees as a first line of defense against winds and drifting snow.

Cooling breezes To trap beneficial summer breezes, create a U-shaped or semicircular planting curved to face the prevailing direction of the breezes. The catch basin will circulate breezes back into the area, making conditions more comfortable. With careful planning, a single planting can reduce winter winds and increase the circulation of summer breezes. A dense stand of trees planted on the northwest side will protect a house from north winds in winter and redirect south winds in summer. See illustration, above.

Shelterbelt and snowcatch In cold-winter regions a shelterbelt helps control wind and blowing snow on large properties. A shelterbelt is created when several rows of tall trees or shrubs are planted perpendicular to the wind. Snowcatches, rows of low shrubs or trees, are often planted with shelterbelts to catch wind-blown snow before it drifts against homes and driveways. Deciduous shrubs and trees together with rows of evergreens are most effective.

Reducing Fire Danger

Because there is so little moisture in the air and in the ground, fire is an ever-present danger in the arid West. The area around your home can be made fire resistant with the proper placement and maintenance of all plants generally, and the use of fire-retardant

species. Don't plant medium-sized shrubs under tree canopies within 50 feet of structures. The shrubs will create a fire ladder into the trees from which flames can jump to the structures. Don't plant large trees so that foliage is within 10 feet of a wall. Avoid planting highly flammable trees such as pine near buildings. If they are already there, remove the lower limbs so that they are less likely to become fire ladders. Mow dry grass and remove brush and tree litter from within 100 feet of structures and from under shrubs.

Many drought-tolerant plants are also useful fire retardants. Generally they have a high moisture content with a low fuel volume (plant material that doesn't burn well). Examples include ice plant (*Mesembryanthemum* and other genera, such as *Carpobrotus, Drosanthemum, Delosperma,* and *Lampranthus*), aloe, agave, and other succulents. In areas where the fire danger is high, a 50-foot band of such plants is recommended around structures. Some plants previously considered to be fire resistant—for example, saltbush (*Atriplex*)—are actually flammable as they mature and accumulate dead wood and litter. Regular pruning of the "dead fuel" reduces flammability.

Check with your local cooperative extension office for advice on which of the plants that grow well in your area show the most fire resistance.

Tending the Garden

As in the rest of the country, soil, temperature, and rainfall determine garden practices in the arid West. Although many standard gardening techniques apply, they must be modified to suit the unique needs of the area.

The techniques of gardening—preparing the soil, fertilizing, planting, and so on—are different in the arid West than they are elsewhere. The lack of rainfall, extremes in temperature, poor soils, and other factors discussed in the first chapter create a set of gardening conditions that dictate a different way of gardening.

This chapter discusses aspects of tending a western garden. In addition to examining soil problems peculiar to the arid West, it explains how and when to improve the soil—as well as when not to improve it. Some amendments and fertilizers are suited to western conditions; others may pose problems. Guidance on what to look for is provided. Some helpful tips on planting, weeding, and pruning are given. There is also advice on protecting plants from the insect and animal pests that plague gardeners in the region. Depending on where your garden is and on your microclimates, you may have to protect plants from the elements. Advice about protecting plants from extremes in temperature and exposure to sun are also provided.

In tending your garden, try to approach each task from a western perspective, using the information in this chapter and your own experience. After a few seasons, you will have a better sense for gardening techniques and a better understanding of your garden site.

Raised planting beds allow for more controlled use of soil amendments and fertilizers, improved drainage, and more efficient use of water.

WESTERN SOILS

Soils are highly variable in the arid West. They can be sandy and fast-draining, as they are in the Coachella Valley of California, or claylike and slow-draining, as they are in most of Colorado and Utah. In some areas there are soil pans or impenetrable layers to contend with. In most areas there is a scarcity of organic matter to work its way into and improve the soil.

The pH scale, numbered from 0 to 14, measures relative acidity or alkalinity. In areas of low rainfall, soils tend to be alkaline, meaning they are above pH 7.0, the neutral point. In areas of higher rainfall, such as parts of northern California, soils are often acidic, or below pH 7.0. The pH of a soil is important to plant growth because it affects the availability of nutrients. Some nutrients, such as iron, become tied up chemically as the soil becomes more alkaline. Problems with salinity (the amount of salt in the soil) also tend to increase with alkalinity. Both acidity and alkalinity can be modified, but if you have a problem that cannot be corrected by any of the methods described below, consider having your soil analyzed. Most states in the West, with the exception of California, will conduct a soil test. Contact your state university or the cooperative extension office in your area for information.

Identifying Your Soil Type

There's a simple way to determine your soil type. Wet a small handful of soil and try to roll it into a cigar shape. Clay will feel smooth; it will form and hold a pencil-thin shape and your hands will be stained a dark color. If the soil feels gritty and immediately crumbles when you try to roll it, it's sandy. If it crumbles before you can get it pencil-thin, it's loamy, which means that it is a desirable mixture of sand, silt, and clay.

Testing the Drainage

Most plants, especially drought-tolerant ones, require good drainage. If soils don't drain well, the root zone becomes saturated with water, leaving no room for air. Plants can suffocate when that happens.

Test intended planting sites to be sure they don't hold water excessively. Dig a hole 2 feet deep by any width (you can dig a narrow hole with a posthole digger) and fill it with water. Allow it to drain completely so that the surrounding soil is saturated. Then fill the hole again and note the drop in the water level. The level should drop at least 6 inches in 24 hours. This rate will provide adequate drainage because the ground is unlikely to receive more than 6 inches of rainfall or watering in a single day. If the level drops less than 6 inches, the soil is draining too slowly and the plant roots might suffocate.

For fast-draining soils, the length of time it takes the water to drain is not as important as the holding capacity of the soil. Some loamy soils may drain rapidly but still hold water in the spaces between soil particles. Very sandy soils will drain quickly, sometimes in a matter of minutes, without retaining much water. Adding organic matter will improve the drainage of most soils.

Adding Organic Matter

In clay soils, organic matter such as composted leaves or ground bark opens up the tight pore spaces and improves aeration, water infiltration, and drainage. In sandy soils, organic matter creates a better mixture of large and small spaces between soil particles, enabling moisture and nutrients to remain longer in the root zone of plants. The beneficial effects wear off, so replenish the supply of organic matter yearly.

Organic matter physically changes the soil structure. The volume of organic matter to add depends on the condition of the soil and

Soil amendments are necessary for many western soils. To make best use of them, first define the area to be amended.

Spread the amendment and turn it evenly into the soil. The result is a thriving vegetable patch in an otherwise arid back yard.

the type of amendment. The more clay based or sandy the soil, the more amendment is needed. Generally, organic matter should make up about one quarter to one third of the amended soil. To improve the soil for a vegetable or flower garden, for example, add about 6 inches of amendment over the planting bed. Thoroughly mix the soil and amendment together to a depth of 18 inches. (In very hard soils, mix it in as deep as you can.) Incorporate it well—there should be no streaks or pockets of amendment to affect root growth. Don't work clay soil when it is wet or it will dry into bricklike clumps. Wait until the soil is barely moist and crumbly.

Soil amendments   Gardeners in arid regions have to be concerned about the salt content of soil. A salty soil amendment can create a saline soil or add to soil salinity. Salinity is a common problem in alkaline soils. Manure, a frequently used amendment that is high in salts, should be added only in small quantities each year. If it is obtained from a feed lot or farm, don't use it until it has aged at least six months or until it loses its strong odor.

Sawdust, bark chips, or other wood products should be well composted or nitrified (supplied with added nitrogen). Soil bacteria need nitrogen to fuel their decomposition of fresh wood. Because there isn't enough nitrogen in the wood itself, the bacteria take it from the soil leaving little or none for plants, resulting in nitrogen drag or depletion. To be on the safe side, many gardeners add extra nitrogen fertilizer when they amend the soil. For more information about nitrogen fertilizers, see page 38.

There are many types of soil amendments available, such as garden compost, ground bark, pine needles, leaf mold, and a variety of locally produced materials. Coarse amendments work better than fine-textured ones in the arid West because they break down more slowly during long seasons of intense heat. Although popular in the East, peat moss is not recommended for hot-summer areas because it dissipates quickly.

When Not to Amend

Sometimes it is better not to amend the soil. Research during the past several years has shown that trees establish themselves and grow better when planted in unamended soil. If the soil in the planting hole is richer than the surrounding native soil, roots will tend to stay there. Planted in unamended soil, trees send out roots far beyond the original planting hole in search of nutrients.

The addition of organic matter can harm or even kill some native plants that thrive in unamended soil. Plants adapted to a particular soil—even if it is extremely rocky or claylike—will establish themselves and grow better if planted in similar soil. Consult a nursery specializing in native plants, a local native plant society, or the state university for detailed information on soil requirements for specific plants.

Soil Problems in the West

Lack of rainfall and the high mineral content of western soils create certain problems that must be corrected before most plants can grow successfully.

Soil pans   A soil pan is an impenetrable layer beneath the soil surface that impedes drainage and root growth. There are different kinds of pans including claypan and hardpan. Caliche, a hard chalklike layer of concentrated soil minerals, is a kind of hardpan common in the desert Southwest. Caliche increases the soil pH, often tying up iron in the soil and making it unavailable to plants.

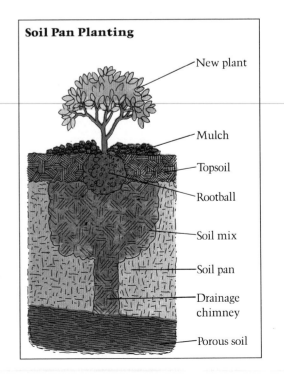

Soil Pan Planting

New plant

Mulch

Topsoil

Rootball

Soil mix

Soil pan

Drainage chimney

Porous soil

If there is a soil pan where you want to grow deep-rooted plants, you must provide water drainage to the subsoil. This can be done by making a chimney—a narrow channel down through the pan to porous soil. Sometimes a heavy iron bar will do the job; in other cases a jackhammer is needed.

Alkaline soils   Soils in arid regions tend to be alkaline, because they contain lime or sodium in quantities high enough to increase the pH to more than 7.0. Gardens irrigated by softened water are also likely to have alkaline soil. Most plants are not bothered by alkalinity until the pH exceeds 8.4—and then nutrients such as iron become tied up and unavailable to plants. Soil sulfur or an ammonium fertilizer will reduce the alkalinity.

Saline soils   Salinity—an accumulation of soluble salts—is a common problem in arid regions. It is particularly troublesome in valleys where salts collect in low-lying areas and there isn't enough rain to wash them down into the soil. Sometimes white salt deposits can be seen on the soil surface. The problem is worse in tight-textured, claylike soils. A high salt content in the local water supply can create or add to a problem of soil salinity. Soils in regions irrigated by the Colorado River are more saline because of the high salt content of the water. Salts can also build up in a garden from repeated use of fertilizers and manure.

Salts are absorbed by plants; in severe cases they prevent seed germination, retard growth, and burn the foliage. The best solution is to leach the soil—apply water slowly for several hours until the salts are washed down past the root zone of the plant. Do this once or twice a year.

Alkali or sodic soils   Alkali soils are the result of low rainfall and poor drainage. They consist of clay soil with enough sodium bonded to the clay particles to interfere with plant growth. (See above for a description of salt damage.) If the soil is well drained and salts don't accumulate, it may be alkali without being saline. To correct an alkali soil, add gypsum (calcium sulfate). The calcium in the gypsum will chemically displace the sodium. Then apply water to leach out the dislodged sodium.

FERTILIZERS

The same organic matter—ground bark, leaf mold, and the like—that improves soil structure also supplies essential plant nutrients. Some gardeners rely solely on organic matter for fertilizer. This may not always work because not all organic matter contributes the same nutrients or has the same effect in soil. The nutrient value of manure, for example, depends on the source and the type of feed that the animal received. In any event, it must be used sparingly because of its high salt content. Other amendments, such as fresh sawdust or bark chips, may cause a problem by depleting the soil of nitrogen. See Soil amendments, opposite page.

To control the nutrient supply more closely, many gardeners use commercial fertilizers in conjunction with organic matter. Every package of commercial fertilizer clearly states the contents. The percentages of three major

Nitrogen-rich plants such as fava bean and Austrian winter pea can be grown during the winter in warmer climates and then turned into the soil to act as "green manure."

Take advantage of otherwise unused space to plant a garden. The warm south wall of this home provides ideal conditions for a mixed flower and vegetable garden.

nutrients—nitrogen, phosphorus, and potassium—appear on the front of the package. These elements are always listed in that order and the absence of any is indicated by a zero. Other nutrients in the fertilizer are listed elsewhere on the package.

Nutrients for Western Soils

Western soils are usually deficient in two of the three major nutrients—nitrogen and phosphorus—but potassium is seldom lacking. Iron, a nutrient required for healthy plant growth, must often be added. Your soil may be lacking in yet other nutrients. If you have a problem affecting plant growth that doesn't fit into the categories listed below, consider a soil test.

Nitrogen   The principal additive in fertilizers is nitrogen because plants need large quantities of it and it is almost always in low supply in the soil. It is rapidly used up by plants or is leached out of the root zone by irrigation water or rainfall. Nitrogen should be applied so that it is available to plants just before and during periods of seasonal growth. Lack of nitrogen causes slowed growth and stunted plants. It also shows up as a yellowing and then dropping of the older leaves, a

condition that spreads tothe whole plant. Many forms of nitrogen are available to home gardeners—organic and synthetic, fast-acting and slow-release.

Phosphorus   Lack of phosphorus is a common deficiency, especially in clay soils and often in red soils. Phosphorus does not have to be replenished as often as nitrogen does because phosphorus does not move in the soil or wash out of the root zone. A phosphorus deficiency slows growth, stunts plants, and results in poor fruit and seed development. Gardeners often add phosphorus in the form of bone meal or superphosphate.

Iron   It is common in alkaline soils to have an iron deficiency. As the soil pH rises, iron becomes tied up chemically. An iron deficiency—iron chlorosis—is indicated by yellowing leaves with veins that remain dark green. Lower the soil pH by adding an acidifying amendment such as soil sulfur, iron sulfate, or an ammonium fertilizer (see opposite page). Iron chelate, a form of iron easily absorbed by plants, can be added to the soil or sprayed on the leaves. Chelates of zinc and manganese are available to correct deficiencies of those elements.

Common Fertilizers in the West

Many different kinds of commercial fertilizers are available to the western gardener. It is a matter of selecting a product that provides the nutrients that your plants need and that your soil lacks. Many gardeners choose an all-purpose fertilizer, often in a 1-1-1 proportion (such as one labeled 10-10-10, meaning 10 percent each nitrogen, phosphorus, and potassium) for general growth or a 1-2-2 proportion (such as 5-10-10) to encourage flowering and fruiting. All-purpose fertilizers—most of which are sold nationally—usually contain potassium because soils in other areas of the United States often need it. Even though potassium is not lacking in western soils, it doesn't hurt to add it.

Ammonium fertilizers   In the arid West ammonium fertilizers are commonly used as a good source of nitrogen and as an acidifier of alkaline soils. Ammonium sulfate, one of the oldest forms of nitrogen fertilizer, contains two acidifying materials: ammonium and sulfur. Since western soils are often deficient in both nitrogen and phosphorus, ammonium phosphate—a fertilizer satisfying both requirements—is also commonly applied. Ammonium

Build raised beds with pressure-treated or rot-resistant wood. Position the drip system and the emitter heads before filling the bed with amended soil and plants.

fertilizers used repeatedly on neutral or slightly acid soils will make them too acidic.

Timing
Fertilize just before the period of new spring growth. Some gardeners fertilize in the fall so that plants do not miss a beat and can draw on nutrients in early spring. Fall feeding can cause problems in colder regions if a flush of new growth occurs just before a cold snap or a damaging frost. In such areas it is best to wait until early spring.

PLANTING
Fall is the best time to set out plants in most areas of the West. The soil is still warm enough to foster root growth, there is ample time for plants to establish themselves before the stress of hot weather, and watering is less critical because winter rains help in this task. In the coldest areas of the West, spring is the favored planting time. Tender plants such as citrus and hibiscus should be planted in spring in all but the warmest winter areas. Palm trees and bamboo, which require warm soil to establish their roots, should be planted in summer through early fall.

Dig planting holes even before buying the plants. Many plants languish or die in their containers waiting for a motivated digger. When deciding between plants in 1-gallon and 5-gallon cans, remember that the smaller, younger plants generally transplant better.

Although the impact of the larger plants is more immediate, the 1-gallon plants catch up to and often surpass them in time.

When planting it is important to space plants according to their size at maturity. Closer placement will mean a crowded garden, higher maintenance, and more pruning.

CONTROLLING WEEDS
In the West the great number of weed species, many of which thrive during mild winters, pose a recurring problem for gardeners. Most weeds can be controlled if they are removed early in their growth cycle, before roots become established and the plant reproduces. Most weeds produce seeds, sometimes thousands at a time. Many of these seeds remain dormant until the soil is cultivated or conditions are favorable for germination. Other weeds reproduce by stolons (aboveground stems) that root wherever they touch the soil, or by extensive rhizomes (underground stems) that can generate new plants all along their length.

Many weeds can be controlled by cultural methods, by herbicides, or by a combination of both. For more information on weed control, refer to Ortho's book *Controlling Weeds*.

Cultural Control
Persistent cultivation at the beginning of the growth cycle discourages many kinds of weeds. Hold the hoe almost parallel to the

Raised beds use space, water, and soil amendments most efficiently, resulting in a more abundant and economical crop.

Fabric mulch retards weed growth while retaining soil moisture. Black fabric will also absorb and retain heat from the sun. Several types of fabric mulch are available.

ground and chop weeds off at the root crown. Don't cultivate deep or you risk bringing more weed seeds to the surface. If hand-pulling weeds, give them a twist and try to get the root as well. During the wet season, pull weeds after a rain when the soil is moist and weeds are easier to remove.

A mulch, either organic or inorganic, around plants or over bare soil helps prevent weeds. In the past it was recommended that plastic sheeting be placed beneath the mulch to hinder weed growth. But, because the plastic must be punctured to allow drainage, water is conveniently funneled down to the weed seeds. It is better to apply a thick layer of mulch, up to 6 inches deep, and to remove weeds when they appear. Another alternative is to lay a mulch of landscape fabric—which is permeable to air and water and does not require puncturing—on the soil and cover that with bark chips, rocks, or other material.

Chemical Control

Sometimes herbicides are necessary, especially if weeds emerge over a large area. Herbicides can be grouped into two general types: preemergent and postemergent. As the name suggests, a preemergent herbicide kills weed seeds before they sprout. It is applied to the

soil before the weed's growth cycle—in early spring throughout the West and also in fall in warm-winter regions. A postemergent herbicide is applied to the weed after it is growing.

Some herbicides are selective and kill only certain kinds of plants. For example, 2,4-D kills only broadleaf plants, leaving grasses alone. Fluazifop-butyl kills only grasses, leaving broadleaf plants alone. Nonselective herbicides, such as glyphosate, kill all the plants they come in contact with.

PRUNING

More gardeners are confounded by pruning probably than by any other gardening task. Western gardeners are no exception. One of the benefits of a water-conserving landscape, however, is its natural appearance. Most plants look best when left to their natural habits. Prune only for a reason: to remove dead or diseased branches, eliminate crossing branches, or to open up a plant that has become too crowded. For pruning techniques see Ortho's book *All About Pruning.*

Pruning Tips

A lot of pruning can be avoided simply by picking the right plant for the right spot. In deciding on the right plant, do not be deterred by labels. Many plants categorized as large shrubs, for instance, can be trained as small trees and vice versa. The mature size of a plant is what matters.

Learn about the pruning needs of various plants. For example, certain plants such as matilija-poppy (*Romneya coulteri*) and Japanese honeysuckle (*Lonicera japonica*) should be pruned back severely each winter. Where applicable, pruning requirements are discussed under Culture in the plant charts, beginning on page 72.

Thin and selectively prune branches of mature, overgrown trees. This will enhance their appearance and reduce the water needs of the plant, because with fewer leaves there is a reduction in transpiration. Pruning is also important if you live where the danger of fire is high. Removing dead wood and litter reduces the flammability of many plants.

Save major pruning cuts for the plant's dormant season, usually late winter to early spring. In low desert regions spring comes very early, so don't wait too long in winter.

PROTECTING PLANTS

To protect plants can mean many things, such as sheltering them from sun, wind, and cold or safeguarding them from insect and animal pests. Protection is most important during the first year, when young plants must put down a good root system and adapt to their growing conditions.

Sun, Wind, and Cold Protection

The best way to overcome the problem of intense sun and strong winds is to select plants that can tolerate these conditions. Consult the plant lists and charts beginning on page 66. The next best way to protect plants from the elements is to provide them with shelter. An understanding of the microclimates in your garden (see page 14) will help you find suitable plants. Measures taken to create shade or to dissipate wind, for example, are other forms of plant protection.

Sun and heat Shade cloth or latticework can be used on a short-term or permanent basis to protect plants from sun and heat. Intense sun can actually sunburn the bark of many plants, particularly citrus. Protect young trees by loosely wrapping the trunk with a tree-wrap material or painting it with white water-soluble paint.

Wind A windbreak may be necessary to protect plants from gusts of cold or hot winds. It can consist of a structure or a band of wind-tolerant plants. See page 30.

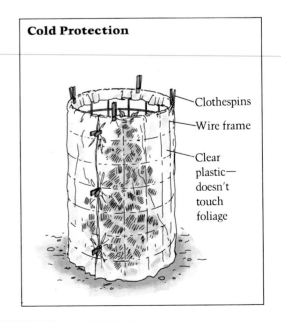

Cold Protection

Clothespins

Wire frame

Clear plastic— doesn't touch foliage

Plastic mesh stretched over a frame of PVC pipe can be used to shade tender lettuce plants from the sun.

Cold frames provide a warm, insulated place for starting early crops or extending the growing season into the winter.

Cold protection Avoid damage by choosing plants that will survive the normal low temperatures in your area. Place tender plants in a warm microclimate, such as under a roof overhang, or grow them in containers and move them to a protected spot when frost threatens.

Freezes can occur in almost every part of the West. Young or tender plants can be protected during most frosts. Cover the plants with blankets, tarps, or plastic. If possible, construct a framework to support the cover, allowing clearance between it and the foliage. It may be worth the trouble to position light bulbs, powered by extension cords plugged into exterior outlets, at the base of valuable, established plants to supply additional heat.

Mulch

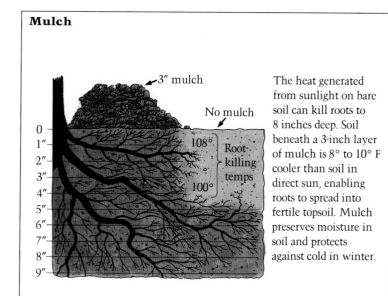

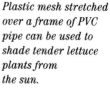

The heat generated from sunlight on bare soil can kill roots to 8 inches deep. Soil beneath a 3-inch layer of mulch is 8° to 10° F cooler than soil in direct sun, enabling roots to spread into fertile topsoil. Mulch preserves moisture in soil and protects against cold in winter.

Clear plastic wrapped around a frame of PVC pipe creates a simple, portable protection against night frosts.

Mounding or wrapping organic mulches such as leaves or peat moss as insulation around trunks and foliage will also help.

Insect Pests

Because of limited rainfall and low humidity, there are fewer insect pests in the arid West. Under the right conditions, however, certain spoilers can wreak havoc on your garden. Some of the major offenders are listed here. For information about other common insects, refer to Ortho's book *Controlling Lawn & Garden Insects.*

Aphids   There are hundreds of different kinds of aphids that attack garden plants. These small, soft-bodied insects vary in color; some have wings. They do their damage by sucking plant juices, particularly from tender, new growth. Control aphids by hosing them off with a blast of water. If the infestation is heavy, spray with an insecticidal soap solution. A contact spray containing diazinon, malathion, or pyrethrins, or insecticide soaps are best for use on edible plants, but may also be used on ornamentals. A systemic spray containing acephate should be used only on inedible ornamentals.

Beetles   The Colorado potato beetle, the June beetle, the cucumber beetle, and the palo verde beetle are among the most common beetles attacking garden plants in the West.

The Colorado potato beetle is devastating when it attacks potato, tomato, eggplant, and pepper plants. The plump, brightly colored beetle, yellow with black stripes, is about ⅓ inch long. Control with an insecticide containing carbaryl or diazinon. When close to harvest time use an insecticide containing pyrethrins.

June beetles are night feeders that eat the leaves of many trees. About 1 inch long, these insects are tan to reddish brown. June beetles are attracted to light, so light traps are effective.

The giant palo verde beetle, which grows up to 3 inches long, is commonly found in the Southwest, usually in midsummer. The grub—the wormlike larva—is usually not seen, because it hides deep in the soil for several years feeding on the roots of palo verde and other deciduous trees. The tree declines in health and entire branches die back. The best control is to squash the big beetles when you see them before they can lay new crops of eggs at the base of host trees.

Grape leaf skeletonizer If you forget to check on your grapevines during the spring and fall, you may find that small, yellow-and-black worms have defoliated them. In spring watch for black, slow-moving moths that resemble wasps and lay eggs on grape leaves. The worms that hatch devour the leaves, giving them a skeletal appearance. Remove and destroy the worms, being careful to keep them away from you because they are a skin irritant. Large colonies can be controlled with a spray containing carbaryl.

Mites Not actually insects, mites are relations of spiders and ticks. Like aphids they come in a variety of colors and are partial to many kinds of plants. They are often red and can be found on the underside of leaves where they suck plant juices. Small silky webs are sometimes visible. Hot, dry weather tends to encourage infestations. Hose off mites with a strong spray from a garden hose. Insecticides are usually needed for larger infestations. Use a dormant oil spray to control mites on woody ornamentals. On herbaceous (nonwoody) ornamentals, apply a chemical containing acephate. Spray edible plants with a chemical containing malathion or diazinon.

Tent caterpillars Often tent caterpillars and their webs are visible in tree branches in spring when new leaves appear. Among their favorite trees are cottonwoods. In spring when the caterpillars are still small, try to remove the webs you can reach with a long-handled broom or brush. Don't touch the caterpillars because they will irritate your skin. Control is easiest when caterpillars are tiny. Use the bacterial spray BT (*Bacillus thuringiensis*) or spray with an insecticide containing acephate, malathion, or carbaryl. Be sure that the spray gets inside the webbing.

Animal Pests

Often animal pests can make short work of a garden. Damage by birds, rabbits, and squirrels is common; in some areas gardeners have to contend with deer, gophers, raccoons, and even javelina (wild pigs). These animals can quickly cause extensive damage, and once accustomed to the offerings of your garden, they will probably return. Scarecrows, windmills, and the like work for only a short time.

Deer The best way to discourage deer is to fence them out with a well-constructed barrier at least 8 feet high. It must be that high because deer are agile jumpers. Electrified wire will work but is more of an undertaking than most gardeners care to deal with. There are such things as deer-resistant plants, although their effectiveness is unpredictable. Very hungry deer will nibble at plants they usually forgo, and the tastes of deer often differ from region to region. It is best to check with a local nursery or the cooperative extension office in your county for recommendations of plants that are considered locally to be deer resistant.

Paint or wrap the trunks of young trees and shrubs to protect them from insects and sunburn.

Steel poles and PVC pipe provide the framework for protective netting designed to keep birds away from vegetables. The clear plastic sheeting can be placed over the frame for protection from frosts at night.

Birds Although birds are an asset in a garden, they can wear their welcome thin by stealing almost all the fruit from fruit trees and vines. An easy way to prevent that, without harming the birds, is to cover the fruiting plants with plastic or nylon netting.

Rabbits Keep rabbits from damaging plants by fencing them out with a mesh fence 2 feet high and buried 6 inches underground. Build a simple wood frame around the garden and attach the mesh to it, or protect individual plants by encircling or covering them with chicken wire or mesh.

Gophers In many parts of the West, gophers are a serious problem. From underground they feed on bulbs and roots, sometimes pulling entire plants down into their tunnels. They can kill shrubs by eating most of the roots and girdling the underground part of the trunk or stems. Gophers leave crescent-shaped mounds of soil on the surface after excavating a new tunnel. They can be controlled by trapping, although the effort can be extremely frustrating. Individual plants such as a newly planted tree can be protected by lining the planting hole with wire mesh. This shields the root sys-

tem during its early development. The bottom and sides of an entire vegetable bed, especially one planted in a raised box, can also be protected in this manner.

Diseases

The normally arid conditions of the West mean that there are fewer plant diseases, just as there are fewer insect pests in the region. A number of diseases prevalent in the region are particularly damaging.

Texas root rot The fungus that causes Texas root rot lives in the warm alkaline soils of California's Imperial and Coachella valleys, Arizona, and New Mexico. It kills by rotting plant roots, and during summer is a common cause of death of woody plants. Afflicted plants wilt rapidly, and their branches retain dead leaves. By the time the disease is detected, it is usually too late to save the plant. You can try to save it by pruning off damaged branches and applying about 2 inches of steer manure on top of the soil, beneath the canopy of the tree or shrub. Cover this with soil sulfur and ammonium sulfate, each applied at the rate of 1 pound per 10 square feet. These amendments acidify the soil and make it less

Mothballs may be useful in keeping mice and snails away from the trunk of a dwarf peach tree.

alkaline. Dig them into the soil and irrigate deeply. If the fungus is a problem in your garden, consult your local cooperative extension office for a list of immune and resistant plants.

Oak root fungus   Also known as armillaria root rot, oak root fungus is a widespread problem in California. The fungus infects a number of plants including oaks. It kills by gradually decaying the roots and moving into the main stem where it girdles the plant. There is often a general withering and yellowing of leaves. The disease can be identified by the appearance of white striated fans of fungus under the bark and between grooves on the bark. Mushrooms often grow around the plant in fall or winter. The fungus is encouraged by moist conditions

during summer in areas that do not normally receive summer rain. To discourage the disease, don't irrigate oaks and other susceptible plants during summer and don't disturb the soil level around the trunk. When removing a diseased plant, be sure to get all the roots or the fungus will remain in the soil. If oak root fungus is a problem in your area, plant immune or resistant species. Consult your local cooperative extension office for a list.

In the vegetable garden   Verticillium and fusarium wilts can be a serious problem in the vegetable garden. Use resistant vegetable varieties where possible. Consult your local nursery for information on controlling powdery mildew, blight, and other vegetable garden diseases.

Watering the Garden

Efficient use of water, whether with traditional watering methods or drip systems, is increasingly important for western gardeners.

Much—often 50 percent or more—of the water consumed by households in the arid West is used in the garden. Unfortunately, most of it is wasted because of inefficient watering.

It's no surprise that water is a resource in peril in the West. Rapid increases in population, normal low precipitation compounded by cyclical drought, and continuous overdrafting of groundwater supplies have forced water consumption to be regulated in many areas. In some communities only commercial landscape installations are affected, but it is only a matter of time before almost everyone will be faced with legislation restricting the size of lawns, the types of plants that can be used, and when and how much water can be applied.

This chapter provides the basics for understanding how to water efficiently. It explains how to recognize when a plant needs water, the importance of encouraging deep roots, and how soil affects watering. It scans through the array of sophisticated components that make up drip systems today and explains how to create a custom-made system suitable for watering all plantings except lawns. For the lawn—the biggest water consumer in the garden—there are practical guidelines for reducing consumption, including a watering schedule based on local evapotranspiration rates.

By following the principles of xeriscape gardening (see pages 18 to 25) and the advice provided in this chapter, anyone can have a water-conserving garden, without having to sacrifice any of the pleasure of gardening.

Drip systems are an economical, flexible, simple, and efficient means of irrigating all plantings except lawns. Automatic timers save time and effort. Some of the many available drip-system components are pictured here.

GIVING PLANTS THE WATER THEY NEED

All plants must be watered regularly until they are established. This usually takes one or two full seasons. Afterward, some plants continue to need frequent irrigation, others need occasional watering, and still others can survive on annual rainfall.

More plants are killed by too much water than by not enough. Overwatered plants are susceptible to diseases. If the soil is saturated for too long, plants can even suffocate and die. The object of proper irrigation is to give plants as much water as they need and only when they show signs of needing it. It is better to stress plants a bit than it is to water too soon. Learn to recognize when a plant needs water and let it go almost to that point before watering. Don't go past that point or the plant may be damaged.

Signs of Water Need

Curling leaves are the first sign of water stress. The plant is reducing its surface area to cut down on transpiration (loss of water from the leaves). Normally shiny leaves grow dull. Bright green leaves take on a blue or gray-green appearance. New growth wilts or droops and older foliage turns brown, dries up, and falls off. Flowers fade quickly and drop off prematurely.

A dry soil surface is not a sign of water need. The surface always dries out first and is not a true indicator. Use a probe or stick to check whether the soil down deep near the plant roots is still moist.

Encouraging Deep Roots

Shallow, frequent irrigation promotes rooting near the soil surface, where moisture is constantly available. Deep, infrequent watering encourages roots to grow down in search of water. Deep roots are better insulated against heat and cold, are anchored better against winds, and have a greater reservoir from which to draw water.

Rooting depth depends on the type of plant. Most conventional lawns root within the top 6 inches of soil; native grasses can grow down 2 feet or more. Annuals and some perennials grow between 1 and 1½ feet deep and shrubs to 3 feet deep. Although trees do have some deep roots, most of the roots are within the top 3 feet of soil. Some species such as mesquite send taproots down 60 feet or deeper.

Once established, the plants in this southern California garden require very little water. Overwatering discourages plants from developing deep roots and is actually harmful for most plants.

Watering Methods

Hand watering is the least efficient method partly because it is difficult to regulate the amount of water being delivered to plants, and partly because many gardeners forget to do it. Portable sprinklers are also difficult to control. Water is usually applied to an area larger than necessary and at a faster rate than the soil can accept.

A conventional underground sprinkler system is the best way to water a lawn. A drip system is the most practical way to water all other plantings.

Applying Water

The best time to irrigate is during the relative cool and calm of the evening or early morning. High temperatures and wind increase the rate at which plants transpire. Wind also blows water away from plants.

Where to apply water is as important as when to apply it. As a plant grows, its root zone also grows and extends out and down. The roots that absorb water—the feeder roots—are concentrated at the outside edges of the plant's drip line (where rainwater drips off leaves to the ground). This is the area that should receive water. Position drip emitters here. If irrigating by hand, build a shallow basin just outside the drip line and apply water in the hollow.

The Effect of Soil Type

The type of soil in your garden greatly affects the rate at which water will get to the root zone and the time it will remain there. The soil

Top: Drip irrigation emitters deliver small, carefully controlled amounts of water just where needed, thereby cutting water use, reducing water runoff, and encouraging deeper plant roots through deeper water penetration.
Bottom: This soaker hose has small holes to allow water to spray slowly and evenly into the soil. It is also portable and may be moved to meet the needs of seasonal plantings, such as spring bulbs. Other types of soaker hose release water more slowly.

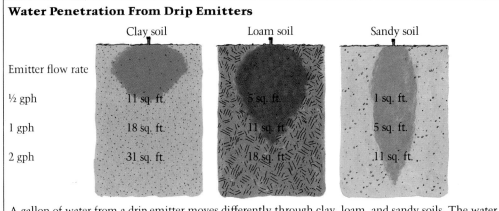

Water Penetration From Drip Emitters

	Clay soil	Loam soil	Sandy soil
Emitter flow rate			
½ gph	11 sq. ft.	5 sq. ft.	1 sq. ft.
1 gph	18 sq. ft.	11 sq. ft.	5 sq. ft.
2 gph	31 sq. ft.	18 sq. ft.	11 sq. ft.

A gallon of water from a drip emitter moves differently through clay, loam, and sandy soils. The water spread increases with the gph* flow rate. Note how much deeper water penetrates in sandy soil. Shaded areas show the wetting pattern.   *gph = gallons per hour

Drip Line

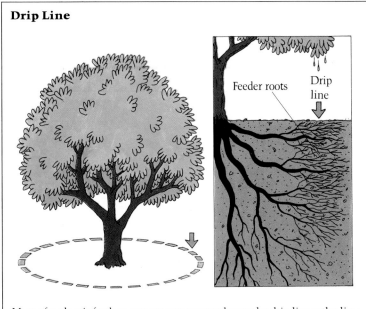

Feeder roots   Drip line

Most of a plant's feeder roots are concentrated near the drip line—the line beneath the outer edge of the plant's foliage.

profile illustrated above shows how water moves differently through different soils.

As a rule, 1 inch of water in a sandy soil will penetrate about 15 inches deep. To reach 3 feet deep, water must be applied slowly for about an hour and a half. In clay soils 1 inch of water will penetrate only 4 to 5 inches deep. Water would have to be applied slowly for about four hours to reach 3 feet deep. Loamy soils fall between the two extremes.

Many gardeners use a shortcut—a deep root irrigator—to get water deep into the soil quickly. The irrigator, consisting of a long thin tube attached to a hose, is inserted into the soil. It is particularly effective on slopes and in heavy clay soils.

WATERING A LAWN

Most of the water used in a garden goes on the lawn and much of this is wasted. In addition to restricting lawn area and using drought-tolerant grasses, it is possible to use water more efficiently.

Use an Efficient Sprinkler

The best way to irrigate a lawn is with an automated conventional spray sprinkler system. If you already have a system but rarely see it in operation because it runs early in the morning, turn it on periodically to make sure that it is working properly. Fix leaks immediately. If the system is older, the heads may emit water faster than the soil can absorb it, resulting in runoff. Low-gallonage spray heads, which emit water more slowly, can be substituted. Heads with a lower trajectory—so that the spray is less likely to be deflected by wind—are also available, as are more efficient nozzle patterns. Older heads often apply the same quantities of water regardless of their spray pattern. Newer heads apply water proportionately—a half-circle head, for example, applies half the water of a full-circle head.

Money spent on installing a more efficient sprinkler system or in upgrading an old system is well spent and will be quickly recovered in lower water bills.

Develop a Watering Schedule

Many water companies in the West are using a system based on the local ET (evapotranspiration) rate to help customers figure out how much to water their lawns. *ET* refers to the amount of water that evaporates from the

Water Harvesting

Rainfall can be harvested for use in the garden instead of being allowed to run down the street or into a sewer. By contouring the terrain, it is possible to funnel rainfall runoff from rooftops, downspouts, and paved surfaces into basins around plants or into rain barrels. A dry creek that is ornamental during dry weather can be used to direct runoff to a collection site. Ditches lined with drain tile can serve the same function. Underground cisterns and tanks can be installed to store rainfall, and water can be pumped for use in the garden during dry periods.

Prevailing wind

NORTH

1. Driveway and walks slope to carry water to lawn areas
2. Water from roof channeled to underground storage tank
3. Water from downspouts channeled through perforated plastic hose to lawn and vegetable garden
4. Lawn slopes toward vegetable garden
5. Berm prevents water runoff from vegetable garden

Test and adjust the evenness of a conventional sprinkler system's coverage by placing flat-bottomed containers on the lawn, running the system, and measuring the amount of water collected in each container.

soil plus the amount that is transpired by the lawn. By knowing how much water was lost, you know how much to replace. Any more water is not used by the lawn and is wasted.

First measure the output from your lawn sprinklers. Distribute several flat-bottomed containers of the same size on the lawn. Run the sprinklers for 15 minutes, then measure to the nearest $1/16$ inch the average depth of water in the containers. If there is more than a $1/4$-inch difference among containers, your sprinkler system needs adjustment.

Taking into account the amount of water in the containers and the grass variety, your local water company or cooperative extension office can provide you with a watering schedule specifying the number and length of weekly irrigations. This schedule will vary seasonally to accommodate temperature, humidity, and other changes.

Rarely should a lawn be watered more than twice a week, even in very hot climates. It is better to water longer than more often. Too frequent watering only encourages shallow rooting and a greater dependence on water.

Lawn Shapes for Watering

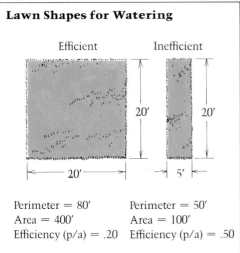

Efficient   Inefficient

Perimeter = 80′	Perimeter = 50′
Area = 400′	Area = 100′
Efficiency (p/a) = .20	Efficiency (p/a) = .50

Make the Lawn An Efficient Shape

Some lawn shapes and sizes lend themselves to efficient irrigation by spray sprinklers; others don't. Curved lawns may be more pleasing to the eye, but rectangles and squares can be irrigated more accurately, with fewer heads and less waste of water. An easy way to calculate the watering efficiency of a lawn is to divide the total perimeter by the square footage. If the perimeter-to-area ratio exceeds .25, the lawn is inefficient. For example, a 20-foot by 20-foot lawn can be watered efficiently (the 80-foot perimeter divided by 400 square feet equals .20) but a 20-foot by 5-foot lawn is inefficient (the 50-foot perimeter divided by 100 square feet equals .50). See the illustration on page 54. Use this formula when reducing a lawn area or establishing a new lawn.

More Water-Saving Tips

These additional hints for conserving water actually reduce maintenance instead of increasing it.

Conduct a stress test Don't water unless it is necessary. You can tell when a lawn is thirsty by walking on it. If footprints remain after a few minutes, the lawn needs water. A green lawn takes on a bluish cast. If a lawn that is not dormant looks brown but the blades bounce back, it may need fertilizer instead.

Punctuate irrigation If the soil is slow to accept water even from low-gallonage spray

heads, program the sprinklers to run for a few minutes, turn off, and then run again. The soil can absorb water more easily this way.

Top: If footprints remain on a dry lawn, it's time to water. Bottom: This garden takes advantage of water runoff from the lawn to irrigate the plantings on and around the patio.

Left and right: Sloping irrigation troughs, a garden hose, and wood shingles have been used to create this simple yet effective system for watering.

Remove thatch   Thatch, an accumulation of dead grass stems, can become almost impenetrable, causing water to run off the lawn. Remove it yearly in late spring using a power rake or dethatcher available at equipment rental shops. It may also be necessary to aerate the lawn by removing small cores of grass and soil to improve water penetration.

Don't overfertilize   Nitrogen fertilizer makes a lawn grow faster and increases its need for water. Fertilize only enough to keep the lawn attractive and it will not be necessary to irrigate as often. A fertilizer schedule depends on the type of grass, growing conditions, and season. Experiment with the amount and timing until you are satisfied.

Mow less often   Less frequent and higher mowing will reduce a lawn's need for water. A longer lawn can hold more water and will develop deeper roots. When a lawn is mowed low its roots are exposed to the sun, causing a rapid loss of moisture. However, don't let the lawn grow more than twice the recommended mowing height or it will be damaged when you try to mow.

DRIP IRRIGATION

The term *drip irrigation* is used to describe any low-pressure system that applies water slowly in a small, confined area. It is also called low-volume or micro-irrigation. Water application is expressed in gallons per hour (gph) rather than in gallons per minute (gpm) as it is for a conventional sprinkler system. A system can combine drip emitters, minisprays, minisprinklers, and misters to irrigate all plantings except lawns.

Why Use Drip Irrigation?

A drip system is the most water-conserving method of irrigation, saving up to 70 percent in outdoor water use. It is economical and easy to install. A key feature of the system is that it applies water very slowly. The soil easily absorbs the water and does not seal up or crust over as it will when water is applied more quickly. Slow, direct application of water to the root zone also promotes deep rooting and healthy plant growth. This method of watering eliminates runoff and cuts down on the amount of water lost through evaporation and overspray.

Because a drip system uses water so slowly, a much larger area can be watered from the same water source than is possible with a conventional sprinkler system. Since the system operates on low pressure, leaks are less critical. A major advantage over conventional systems is flexibility. It is easy to add on to or reroute a drip system.

Although it clearly has many benefits, drip systems do have disadvantages—but none that can't be overcome with some care and vigilance. A drip system is subject to clogs and leaks and should be checked regularly. Because not enough water is applied to wash down salts that accumulate in saline soils or that build up from fertilizer or manure, it is usually necessary to leach the soil periodically (see page 37).

Designing a Drip System

Begin by laying out the garden on grid paper. Sketch the areas that you want to irrigate, indicating water source, different kinds of plants, any elevation changes, and pathways and other obstacles that the tubing will have to get around. Accurate measurements will help determine the length of tubing and the number of emitters and fittings needed. Many irrigation supply stores will help you to select the components that will work best for your situation.

If plants are grouped by water need (see page 18), the system will be easier to set up. A very small system can be attached to a hose bib and automated with a battery-operated timer. A larger system can have several lines or circuits, as long as there is a separate valve for each. For example, you could have four circuits to serve a vegetable garden, a row of fruit trees, several flower beds, and a mixed planting of ground covers and shrubs.

Since drip systems use so little water, it is not usually necessary to worry about exact water consumption on each valve. If you have a very large garden or plan to exceed 200 gph on a single circuit, discuss your plans with the irrigation equipment supplier to make sure that enough water is available.

Installation begins at the water source and works out to the emitters. The head assembly—the components that are attached to the water source—consists of a valve, a backflow preventer, a filter, a pressure regulator, and an optional fertilizer injector. The main line leading from this assembly can branch into several lateral lines to carry water to different groups of plants. The lines can be buried in the soil (if burrowing animals are not a problem in your area) and hidden beneath mulch or behind plants.

Drip Irrigation System

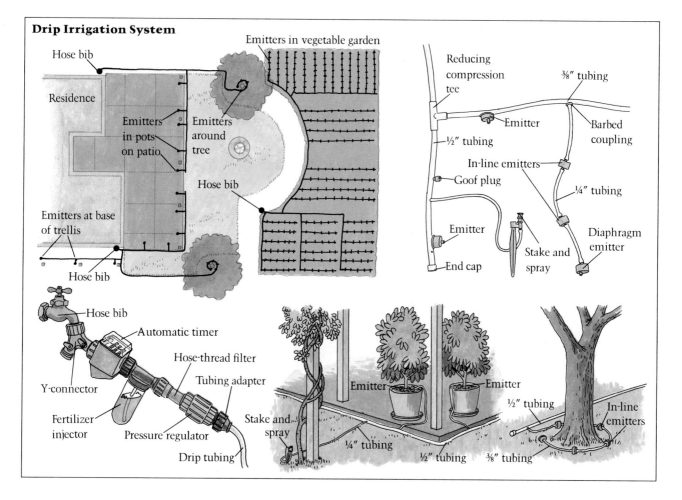

The wide variety of drip components available allows for custom-designed, modifiable watering systems.
Left: Pictured are drip tubing, emitters, valves, and soaker hose.
Right: Here are goof plugs, tubing, misters, joints, adaptors, and other components.

Holes are punched into the main or lateral lines and emitters inserted directly or attached to microtubing leading from the lines. A drip system is extremely flexible because emitters can be removed at any time and goof (stopper) plugs used to seal the holes. In that way one or more plants in a grouping can be taken off the drip system without affecting the rest of the line. The plugs can easily be taken out and emitters snapped in again.

The illustrations on page 57 show how a typical drip system is put together. The components are described below.

Emitters

There are many more types of emitters today than there were when drip systems first came on the market. The plants and terrain usually determine the type of emitter used.

Drip emitters Usually available for flow rates of ½ to 4 gph, these emitters drip water on individual plants such as trees, shrubs, and container plants. Emitters with different flow rates can be used on the same system. Most emitters have barbed ends that snap into punched holes in ½- or ⅜-inch tubing or that may be pushed into ¼-inch microtubing. Pressure-compensating emitters provide a steady flow rate; use them if there is an elevation change of over 10 feet, if lateral lines exceed 200 feet, or if emitters on a line total more than 100 gph.

Misters These spray water at 2 to 5 gph. Use their fine spray on ferns and other plants that require frequent, light irrigation or high humidity. Even slight breezes can carry water away, so operate them in the early morning and in protected areas. Misters are useful in a propagation area, if you grow your own plants from seeds and cuttings.

Minisprays These come in several spray patterns—90, 180, 300, and 360 degrees as well as patterns for watering narrow strips—and throw water over distances of 4 to 10 feet. Flow rates vary between 3 and 30 gph. Minisprays are positioned 10 to 15 inches above the soil and are held by a stake. They are used for ground covers, flower beds, and vegetables.

Minisprinklers These spinners emit larger droplets than those from minisprays. They distribute water at a rate of 4 to 45 gph in a full circle from 10 to 30 feet in diameter. Minisprinklers are useful in large beds and ground-cover areas.

Microspray nozzles Microspray nozzles use conventional sprinkler system components, such as underground PVC pipe and pop-up spray sprinklers. The microspray nozzle replaces the standard nozzle on a pop-up sprinkler and applies one tenth of the water over the same area.

Other Components

Most of the components listed below are required; the fertilizer injector, soil moisture sensor, and rain sensor are optional.

System shut-off valve This controls the water to the entire drip system. It allows you to add on to the system or repair it without having to turn off the water to the house.

Controller A multiprogram automatic controller allows each valve to be operated independently. Since drip systems apply water slowly, it is best to have a clock that may be programmed in hours as well as in minutes.

Circuit valve Manual, low-flow electric, or battery-operated valves can be used. Electric and manual valves are usually combined with an antisiphon backflow preventer—a device required by most water districts. A battery-operated electronic timer combines the functions of a valve and controller. It requires a separate backflow preventer. Although not as reliable or long lasting as an electric or manual valve, it is automatic and needs no wiring.

Fertilizer injector This device provides a convenient way to feed plants. Frequent dilute feedings are better than several larger feedings. However, fertilizer salts can clog emitters and build up on the soil.

Filter Even where water is generally free of sediment, the occasional particle flushed loose is enough to clog an emitter. Use a filter with a 150- to 200-mesh stainless steel or fiberglass screen. Y-filters are better than in-line filters, because you don't have to take the system apart to clean them.

Pressure regulator Drip systems operate at a water pressure of 20 to 30 pounds per square inch (psi). Since house water ranges from 50 to 100 psi, or even higher in some parts of the West, this device is needed to reduce and regulate the pressure.

Tubing Polyethylene tubing in ½-inch and ⅜-inch diameters is used to distribute water throughout the system. It is flexible, sold in coils, and easy to cut and connect without glue or clamps. PVC pipe is sometimes used for main lines, especially under walkways, and polyethylene tubing for lateral lines. PVC is a better choice for buried lines; polyethylene tubing can be damaged by burrowing animals.

Microtubing This ¼-inch-diameter tubing is used to deliver water from the main tubing

This type of soaker hose sweats water in fine drops, delivering water slowly and evenly.

This hose emits a fine spray of water from small holes.

to the plants. Because it is easier to conceal than is the larger tubing, it is often used to distribute water to containers and hanging baskets. Microtubing with perforations in it is sold as soaker or laser tubing and is commonly used to water rows of vegetables and flowers.

Fittings Compression tees, elbows, and connectors are used to join two pieces of tubing, to split tubing off into different lines, and to make turns. Barbed fittings are used to join microtubing to the main tubing.

Soil-moisture sensor When the sensor detects adequate soil moisture, it overrides the controller and turns off the irrigation cycle.

Rain sensor Mount this device on the eave of the house or somewhere else in the open. After it has accumulated about ⅛ inch of rain, the rain sensor overrides the drip system.

Plant Selection Guide

You don't have to give up color and variety to garden in a dry climate. The many ornamental and edible plants native to the West, and the many more that have been introduced from around the world, offer an abundance of species for all uses.

These are exciting times for western gardeners. Until fairly recently, familiar but thirsty plants adapted to rainy climates were the standard fare at most nurseries. Now the choice is expanding rapidly as nurseries respond to the demand for plants that require less water.

Water-conserving plants are available to fulfill every garden function, from controlling erosion, to providing spectacular color, to creating shade quickly. See the lists, beginning on page 66, of plants for special functions. Charts with descriptions of plants and their cultural requirements begin on page 72. Here old favorites, such as juniper and rosemary, appear with newer names, such as indigo bush (*Dalea* species) and fairy-duster (*Calliandra* species). The charts are organized by plant categories—ground covers, shrubs, trees, and so on—but do not be deterred by labels. You may find an ideal ground cover in the Shrubs chart or a large background shrub in the Trees chart. Make sure that the plant is adapted to your climate because it will grow better and be healthier. Climate zones are described in the first chapter and the zones in which each plant will grow are listed in the Adaptation column of the charts.

The color in this northern California garden comes entirely from drought-tolerant native and adapted perennials—sage, cat's-claw, echium, and the bright purple of wallflowers and snapdragons.

COLOR IN THE GARDEN

Plants have many ways of adding color to a garden—with their flowers, fruit, foliage, and bark. Annuals and perennials are the workhorses of the garden when it comes to providing color. Trees, shrubs, ground covers, and vines can be used just as effectively for seasonal interest. The brilliant orange fruit suspended from the bare branches of a persimmon tree (*Diospyros kaki*) provide welcome color in late fall and early winter. The foliage of some plants, such as Chinese pistache (*Pistacia chinensis*), turns vibrant shades of crimson and orange in the fall. Other plants, such as purple-leaf plum (*Prunus cerasifera* 'Atropurpurea'), retain their brilliance the year around. Western redbud (*Cercis occidentalis*) provides a constant show of color: magenta flowers in spring, red bean pods in summer, yellow or red foliage in fall, and a tangle of bare red-brown branches in winter.

With the increasing number of plants available, there is no need to sacrifice color to conserve water. Every plant selected should be able to provide color in the garden.

Annuals and Perennials

Flowering annuals and perennials are the most popular ways of adding color to the garden. Natives and plants introduced from dry climates around the world offer western gardeners many choices for a water-efficient garden. Some are old favorites—for example, cosmos, yarrow (*Achillea*), and verbena.

Annuals—plants that bloom, set seed, and die in one year or less—are used often because they are short-lived. By replacing annuals it is easy to change the color scheme of the garden. Some annuals perform better during cool weather and should be planted for spring or fall bloom. Others accept high heat and should be planted for summer bloom. Refer to the plant charts beginning on page 72 for blooming times. In warm-winter areas, some annuals live over as perennials.

Perennials are longer-lived plants that usually bloom once a year for from a week to a month, although some bloom throughout their growing season. Some perennials die to the ground yearly and new growth emerges in spring. Other perennials may need to be divided every few years as the clump grows larger and the middle dies out.

Top: The drought-resistant plant palette offers as much color as do more water-demanding plant palettes. All the plants pictured require little or no water to thrive. Bottom: This yucca has its own subtle beauty.

Tender perennials are usually grown as annuals in cold-winter areas. Keep cold tolerance in mind when selecting plants. For example, gazania—which is hardy to 20° F—will die in areas where winter temperatures are lower.

Wildflowers

Wildflowers are native plants that grow in a casual untended environment such as a wildflower meadow. They include annuals and perennials and are a good choice for seasonal color on the outer reaches of a garden.

Wildflower mixes are available at nurseries and through mail-order catalogs. Mixes are often formulated for a general region, such as the high plains or the Southwest desert. Select a mix that is the closest match to your climate and soil conditions. The more specific the mix, the more plants will germinate and survive from year to year.

GROWING VEGETABLES

Whether the harvest itself or the pleasure of producing it is important, edible plants have a place in the arid environment—often as part of a high-water-use zone. Included in this chapter is a chart for vegetables, specifying planting times in the various climate zones. Some vegetables grow better during cool weather; others need heat. Most cool-season vegetables are leaf and root crops—for example, cabbage, onions, and lettuce. Practically all warm-season vegetables are harvested for their fruit, such as tomatoes, cucumbers, melons, and squash.

In mild-winter climates there are two vegetable-planting seasons, one in the spring and one in the fall. Certain crops can be planted the year around in certain climate zones. In cold-winter climates there is usually one growing season beginning in early spring. Sometimes vegetables can be planted in summer for fall harvest if the growing season is long—as in Salt Lake City where it is more than 190 days.

In hot desert regions plants should be established before the heat of summer when temperatures will be rising to 100° F and more. Selecting early maturing varieties helps; look for these in seed catalogs. In desert areas gardeners often must shade their crops from the intense sun and heat. Even in cooler regions such as coastal California, gardeners use shade

Top: The flowering cholla is one of the most beautiful sights in the desert.
Center: With the help of raised beds, efficient drip watering, and cold frames, gardeners in the milder areas of the West can grow plants the year around.
Bottom: Unframed mounded beds allow the gardener to move and replant beds to accommodate different vegetables at various times of the year. A winter planting of lettuce and onions is framed by ripe persimmons (right) and broccoli.

Top: Kale (a relative of cabbage) is a hardy, colorful fall and winter vegetable.
Center: Although small, this hot, south-facing plot provides ideal conditions for growing corn and zucchini.
Bottom: Planted close together to cut down on the evaporation of precious water from the soil are (top to bottom) red brussels sprouts, cabbage, carrots, and Swiss chard.

cloth during unseasonable hot spells to keep cool-weather crops, such as lettuce and peas, from bolting or going to seed.

GROWING FRUIT

More varieties of fruits, berries, and nuts can be grown in the West than in any other part of the United States. The chart on page 70 shows varieties that grow best in each climate zone. A local nursery or the cooperative extension office in your area can also provide advice on what grows well in your area.

Deciduous fruits, such as apple, pear, and peach, require a certain number of chilling hours—hours during the winter when the temperature falls below 45° F. Most need between 500 and 1,000 chilling hours. Fruits that require chilling generally fall into one of three categories.

☐ Low chill: 300 to 400 hours below 45° F
☐ Moderate chill: 400 to 700 hours below 45° F
☐ High chill: 700 to 1000 hours below 45° F

Check the chilling requirement of a particular fruit before buying a plant. Be sure to ask about the increasing number of low-chill varieties that are being developed for mild-winter areas.

Citus

Citus

Citus is grown in Arizona and California wherever temperatures do not fall much below 20° F. The prime growing areas are the interior valleys of California, southern California, and the low deserts of California and Arizona.

Lemons, limes, and other sour citus that require only moderate heat can be grown in cooler climates such as that of coastal northern California. Prolonged periods of heat are needed to form sugar in oranges and other sweet citus. Grapefruit, which needs the most heat, grows best in the hot desert. Citus is affected by seasonal fluctuations of temperature. For most varieties growth ceases below 55° F and above 100° F. The best temperatures for growth are between 70° and 90° F.

Citus bark sunburns easily, especially in the intense light of the low deserts. Protect the trunk with tree wrap or by painting it with white water-soluble paint. In these areas citus should be grown as a large shrub with branches to the ground: The canopy provides shade and frost protection, humidity remains higher under the low branches, and fruit is easier to pick.

Citus is best planted in spring after the last frost date, so that it can establish itself before winter. It prefers constant moisture and a dry trunk, so a drip system is the ideal way of watering. Any departure from a regular regime of watering and fertilizing can cause citus to drop its leaves.

For a complete guide to citus, refer to Ortho's book *All About Citus & Subtropical Fruits*.

Citus varieties from hardiest to least hardy:
Kumquat (tolerant to minimum 18° F)
Orangequat
Sour orange
'Meyer' lemon
'Rangpur' lime
Mandarin orange (tangerine)
Sweet orange
'Bearss' lime
Tangelo
Lemon
Grapefuit
Limequat
'Mexican' lime (tolerant to minimum 28° F)

Top to bottom:
navel oranges,
'Eureka' lemons,
and 'Marsh'
grapefruit.

Plants for Specific Uses

The following lists will help you select plants to serve specific functions in the water-conserving garden. All of the plants included in these lists require little or no water once established. Information about them is listed in the plant charts beginning on page 72.

WINDBREAKS
Brachychiton populneus (bottle tree)
Callistemon citrinus (lemon bottlebrush)
Calocedrus decurrens (California incense-cedar)
Cedrus species (cedar)
Cercidium species (palo verde)
Cupressus arizonica and *glabra* (Arizona cypress)
Dodonea viscosa (hopbush)
Elaeagnus angustifolia (Russian-olive)
Elaeagnus pungens (thorny elaeagnus)
Eucalyptus species (eucalyptus)
Juniperus species (juniper—tall shrubs and trees)
Leptospermum laevigatum (Australian tea-tree)
Ligustrum lucidum (glossy privet)
Maclura pomifera (Osage-orange)
Melaleuca quinquenervia (cajeput-tree, paperbark-tree)
Nerium oleander (oleander)
Pinus species (pine)
Pittosporum species (pittosporum)
Quercus agrifolia (coast live oak)
Rhus ovata (sugarbush)
Schinus molle (California pepper tree)
Sophora secundiflora (Texas mountain laurel, mescal-bean)

FAST-GROWING TREES
Acacia species (acacia)
Acer saccharinum (silver maple)
Callistemon citrinus (lemon bottlebrush)
Casuarina stricta (beefwood)
Catalpa speciosa (western catalpa)
Cedrus deodara (deodar cedar)
Cercidium species (palo verde)
Cupressus arizonica and *glabra* (Arizona cypress)
Eriobotrya japonica (loquat)
Eucalyptus species (eucalyptus)
Gleditsia triacanthos (honey locust)
Grevillea robusta (silk-oak)
Ligustrum lucidum (glossy privet)
Maclura pomifera (Osage-orange)

Melaleuca species (melaleuca)
Parkinsonia aculeata (Mexican palo verde)
Pinus eldarica (eldarica pine)
Schinus molle (California pepper)

EROSION CONTROLS
Aesculus californica (California buckeye)
Atriplex species (saltbush)
Ceanothus species (ceanothus)
Cistus species (rockrose)
Coprosma × *kirkii* (coprosma)
Cotoneaster species (cotoneaster)
Eriogonum fasciculatum (California buckwheat)
Fallugia paradoxa (Apache-plume)
Hypericum calycinum (St.-Johnswort)
Juniperus species (juniper)
Lantana species (lantana)
Lonicera japonica (Japanese honeysuckle)
Mahonia repens (creeping mahonia)
Romneya coulteri (matilija-poppy)
Rosmarinus officinalis 'Prostratus' (dwarf or prostrate rosemary)

PLANTS THAT ATTRACT BIRDS
Albizia julibrissin (silk tree)
Arbutus unedo (strawberry-tree)
Arctostaphylos species and cultivars (manzanita)
Berberis darwinii (barberry)
Celtis species (hackberry)
Cercidium species (palo verde)
Coreopsis tinctoria (calliopsis)
Cosmos bipinnatus (cosmos)
Cotoneaster species (cotoneaster)
Diospyros kaki (oriental persimmon)
Elaeagnus angustifolia (Russian-olive)
Elaeagnus pungens (silverberry)
Eriobotrya japonica (loquat)
Feijoa sellowiana (pineapple guava)
Lantana species (lantana)
Ligustrum lucidum (glossy privet)
Lonicera japonica (Japanese honeysuckle)
Mahonia repens (creeping mahonia)
Melaleuca species (melaleuca)
Penstemon species (penstemon)
Pyracantha species (firethorn)
Rosmarinus officinalis 'Prostratus' (dwarf or prostrate rosemary)
Schinus species (California, Brazilian pepper)
Shepardia argentea (silver buffaloberry)

Vitus species (grape)
Zauschneria species (California fuchsia, hummingbird flower)

HEAT-RESISTANT PLANTS FOR SOUTH AND WEST EXPOSURES
Bougainvillea species (bougainvillea)
Caesalpinia species (bird-of-paradise)
Calliandra species (fairy-duster)
Callistemon citrinus (lemon bottlebrush)
Coprosma × *kirkii* (coprosma)
Distictis buccinatoria (blood-red trumpet vine)
Elaeagnus species (elaeagnus)
Fallugia paradoxa (Apache-plume)
Juniperus species (juniper)
Lantana species (lantana)
Macfadyena unguis-cati (cat's-claw vine)
Nerium oleander (oleander)
Pittosporum species (pittosporum)
Prunus caroliniana (Carolina cherry-laurel)
Punica granatum (pomegranate)
Pyracantha species (firethorn)
Tecomaria capensis (cape honeysuckle)
Wisteria species (wisteria)
Xylosma congestum (shiny xylosma)
Yucca species (yucca)

LOW-LITTER PLANTS SUITABLE FOR POOL AREAS
Aloe saponaria (African aloe)
Amaranthus tricolor (Joseph's coat)
Aspidistra elatior (cast-iron plant)
Cordyline australis (dracaena)
Dietes vegeta (fortnight-lily)
Hemerocallis species (daylily)
Juniperus species (juniper)
Kniphofia uvaria (red-hot-poker)
Raphiolepis indica (Indian-hawthorn)
Yucca species (yucca)

ROCK-GARDEN PLANTS
Achillea species (yarrow)
Armeria maritima (sea pink)
Aurinia saxatilis (basket-of-gold)
Calliandra species (fairy-duster)
Ceanothus species (ceanothus)
Cerastium tomentosum (snow-in-summer)
Ceratostigma plumbaginoides (dwarf plumbago)
Cistus species (rockrose)
Cotoneaster species (cotoneaster)
Dalea greggii (dalea)

Delosperma nubigenum
(ice plant)
Erigeron karvinskianus
(fleabane)
Festuca ovina var. *glauca*
(blue fescue)
Helianthemum nummularium
(sunrose)
Juniperus species (juniperus)
Lantana montevidensis (trailing
lantana)
Lobularia maritima (sweet
alyssum)
Oenothera berlandieri (Mexican
evening primrose)
Penstemon species (penstemon)
Phlox subulata (moss pink)
Rosmarinus officinalis 'Prostratus'
(dwarf or prostrate rosemary)
Salvia species (sage)
Santolina chamaecyparissus
(lavender cotton)
Teucrium chamaedrys
(germander)
Thymus species (thyme)
Verbena species (verbena)
Zauschneria californica
(California fuchsia, hummingbird
flower)

COLOR BY SEASON
Spring
Acacia species (acacia)
Arctotis hybrids (African daisy)
Aurinia saxatilis (basket-of-gold)
Bougainvillea species
(bougainvillea)
Calendula officinalis (calendula)
Callistemon citrinus (lemon
bottlebrush)
Cassia artemisioides
(feathery cassia)
Catalpa speciosa (western catalpa)
Ceanothus species (ceanothus)
Cercidium species (palo verde)
Cercis occidentalis
(western redbud)
Chilopsis linearis (desert willow)
Cistus species (rockrose)
Cowania mexicana (cliffrose)
Dimorphotheca sinuata (cape
marigold)
Distictis buccinatoria (blood-red
trumpet vine)
Fallugia paradoxa (Apache-
plume)
Gazania species (gazania)

Helianthemum nummularium
(sunrose)
Lobularia maritima (sweet
alyssum)
Lonicera japonica (Japanese
honeysuckle)
Parkinsonia aculeata (Mexican
palo verde)
Phlox subulata (moss pink)
Rosa banksiae (Lady Banks rose)
Rosmarinus officinalis 'Prostratus'
(dwarf or prostrate rosemary)
Solanum jasminoides
(potato vine)
Sophora secundiflora (Texas
mountain laurel, mescal-bean)
Wisteria species (wisteria)

Summer
Achillea species (yarrow)
Albizia julibrissin (silk tree)
Bougainvillea species
(bougainvillea)
Caesalpinia species (bird-of-
paradise)
Calliandra species (fairy-duster)
Callistemon citrinus (lemon
bottlebrush)
Catalpa species (catalpa)
Catharanthus roseus (Madagascar
periwinkle)
Centaurea cyanus (bachelor's-
button)
Cerastium tomentosum
(snow-in-summer)
Cercis occidentalis (western
redbud)
Coreopsis tinctoria (calliopsis)
Cosmos bipinnatus (cosmos)
Cowania mexicana (cliffrose)
Distictis buccinatoria (blood-red
trumpet vine)
Eucalyptus ficifolia
(red-flowering gum)
Fallugia paradoxa
(Apache-plume)
Gaillardia × *grandiflora*
(blanketflower)
Gazania species (gazania)
Hemerocallis hybrids (daylily)
Kniphofia uvaria (red-hot-poker)
Lagerstroemia indica
(crape myrtle)
Lantana species (lantana)
Limonium perezii (sea lavender)
Lobularia maritima (sweet
alyssum)

Nerium oleander (oleander)
Polygonum aubertii (silver-
lace vine)
Romneya coulteri (matilija-poppy)
Salvia leucantha (Mexican
bush sage)
Yucca aloifolia (Spanish-bayonet)
Yucca elata (soaptree yucca)

Fall
Calendula officinalis (calendula)
Callistemon citrinus (lemon
bottlebrush)
Catharanthus roseus (Madagascar
periwinkle)
Cercis occidentalis (western
redbud)
Diospyros kaki (oriental
persimmon)
Distictis buccinatoria (blood-red
trumpet vine)
Gaillardia × *grandiflora*
(blanketflower)
Ginkgo biloba (maidenhair-tree)
Liquidambar styraciflua
(sweet gum)
Lobularia maritima (sweet
alyssum)
Nerium oleander (oleander)
Oenothera berlandieri (Mexican
evening primrose)
Osteospermum fruticosum
(trailing African daisy)
Pistacia chinensis (Chinese
pistache)
Salvia greggii (autumn sage)

Winter
Arbutus unedo (strawberry-tree)
Calendula officinalis (calendula)
Cassia artemisiodes (feathery
cassia)
Cercis occidentalis (western
redbud)
Dimorphotheca sinuata
(cape marigold)
Diospyros kaki (oriental
persimmon)
Hakea laurina (pincushion tree)
Leptospermum scoparium 'Ruby
Glow' (tea-tree)
Lobularia maritima (sweet
alyssum)
Osteospermum fruticosum
(trailing African daisy)
Prunus cerasifera 'Atropurpurea'
(purpleleaf plum)

Planting Times for Vegetables in the Arid West

Vegetable	Plant as	Zone 1	Zone 2	Zone 3	Zone 4	Zone 5a
Asparagus	Roots	Apr-May	Apr-May	Apr	Nov-Mar	Nov-Mar
Beans	Seeds	June	June	May-June	Apr-June	Apr-July
Beets	Seeds	May-June	May-June	Apr-June	Apr-June	Apr-Sept
Broccoli	Plants	Apr-June	Apr-June	Apr-May	Mar, Aug	Aug-Mar
Brussels sprouts	Plants	May-June	May-June	Mar-May	Aug-Oct	Sept-Oct
Cabbage	Plants	May-June	May-June	Mar-May	Jan-Feb, July	Sept-Oct
Carrots	Seeds	May-July	May-July	May-July	May-June	Mar-June, Sept-Oct
Cauliflower	Plants	May-June	May-June	Mar-May	July-Nov	Sept-Oct
Celery	Plants	June-July	June-July	May	June-Aug	Sept
Corn	Seeds	June	June	May-June	May-June	Mar-July
Cucumbers	Seeds	May-June	May-June	May-June	May-June	Apr-June
Eggplant	Plants	May-June	May-June	May-June	May-June	Apr-June
Endive	Seeds	Apr-June	Apr-June	Apr-May	Apr-May	Mar-Apr
Lettuce	Seeds	Mar-Aug	Mar-Aug	Mar-Apr, Aug	Mar-Apr, Aug	Aug-Mar
Melons	Seeds	May-June	May-June	May-June	May-June	Apr-June
Onions	Seeds	Mar	Mar	Mar	Nov-Feb	Feb-Mar
	Sets	Apr-May	Apr-May	Mar-May	Feb-Apr	Oct-Apr
Parsley	Seeds	Apr-May	Apr-May	Apr-May	Apr-May	Apr-June
Peas	Seeds	Feb-May	Feb-May	Feb-May	Feb-Apr, Sept	Mar-Apr, Sept-Oct
Peppers	Plants	May	May	May	May-June	Mar-June
Potatoes	Sets	May	May	Apr-May	Dec-Mar	Feb-June
Pumpkins	Seeds	June	June	June	Apr-June	Apr-June
Radishes	Seeds	Apr-June	Apr-June	Apr-June	Mar-May, Sept-Oct	Mar-May, Sept-Oct
Rhubarb	Roots	Mar-Apr	Mar-Apr	Mar-Apr		Jan
Spinach	Seeds	Apr-May	Apr-May	Apr-May	Apr-May	May, Sept-Nov
Squash	Seeds	May-June	May-June	Apr-June	Mar-June	Mar-June
Swiss chard	Seeds	Mar-June	Mar-June	Mar-June	Mar-Apr, Aug	Mar, Aug-Sept
Tomatoes	Plants	May-June	May-June	May-June	Apr-July	Apr-July
Turnips	Seeds	Apr-May	Apr-May	Mar-May	Mar-May	Mar-Apr, Sept-Oct

Zone 5b	Zone 6	Zone 7	Zone 8	Zone 9	Zone 10	Approx. Days to Harvest
Oct–Feb	Oct–Feb		Feb–Apr		Feb–Apr	2 years
Mar–Aug	Mar–Aug	July–Aug	May–June	July–Aug	May–June	50–100
year around	year around	Sept–Mar	Mar–May	Sept–Mar	Mar–May	45–65
Oct–Feb	Oct–Feb	Sept–Dec	Apr–July	Sept–Dec	Apr–July	50–100
Oct–Feb	Oct–Feb	Sept–Dec	July–Aug	Sept–Dec	July–Aug	80–100
Oct–Jan	Oct–Jan	Sept–Dec	Mar–May	Sept–Dec	Mar–May	50–100
year around	year around	Sept–Mar	Mar–May, Aug–Sept	Sept–Mar	Mar–May, Aug–Sept	50–80
Sept–Feb	Sept–Feb	Sept–Dec	Mar–May	Sept–Dec	Mar–May	55–100
Aug–Oct	Aug–Oct	Aug–Oct	May–June	Aug–Oct	May–June	105–130
Mar–July	Mar–July	Mar–Apr	May–July	Mar–Apr	May–July	60–100
Mar–July	Mar–July	Aug–Sept, Dec–Mar	May–June	Aug–Sept, Dec–Mar	May–June	50–70
Mar–June	Mar–June	Feb–May	May–June	Feb–May	May–June	60–95
Apr–June, Oct–Jan	Apr–June, Oct–Jan	Sept–Feb	Feb–Mar	Sept–Feb	Feb–Mar	70–100
Sept–Mar	Sept–Mar	Sept–Apr	Feb–Mar, July–Aug	Sept–Apr	Feb–Mar, July–Aug	40–90
Apr–July	Apr–July	Feb–June	May–June	Feb–June	May–June	70–115
Nov–Feb Oct–Apr	Nov–Feb Oct–Apr	Nov–Feb Oct–Apr	Nov–Apr	Nov–Feb Oct–Apr	Nov–Apr	130–185 95–125
Apr–June, Oct–Jan	Apr–June, Oct–Jan	Sept–Jan	May–June	Sept–Jan	May–June	70–90
Sept–Jan	Sept–Jan	Aug–Mar	Feb–Mar, July–Aug	Aug–Mar	Feb–Mar, July–Aug	55–70
Mar–July	Mar–July	Feb–May	May–June	Feb–May	May–June	60–95
Mar–May, July–Aug	Mar–Apr	July–Aug, Nov–Jan	Mar–July	July–Aug, Nov–Jan	Mar–July	90–110
Apr–June	Apr–June	Apr–Aug	May–June	Apr–Aug	May–June	90–120
year around	year around	Sept–Apr	Mar–Apr, July–Sept	Sept–Apr	Mar–Apr, July–Sept	22–70
Nov–Feb	Nov–Feb		Mar–Apr		Mar–Apr	1 year
Sept–Feb	Sept–Feb	Sept–Mar	Feb–Mar, July–Aug	Sept–Mar	Feb–Mar, July–Aug	40–50
Mar–July	Mar–July	May–Aug, Dec–Mar	May–July	May–Aug, Dec–Mar	Mar–July	50–65
Aug–Mar	Aug–Mar	Sept–Mar	Feb–Apr, July–Sept	Sept–Mar	Feb–Apr, July–Sept	50–60
Apr–July	Apr–July	Jan–Mar	May–June	Jan–Mar	May–June	50–90
year around	year around	Aug–Mar	Mar	Aug–Mar	Mar	30–60

Cantaloupe

Adaptation of Common Fruits, Berries, and Nuts in the Arid West

	Zone 1	Zone 2	Zone 3	Zone 4	Zone 5a	Zone 5b	Zone 6	Zone 7	Zone 8	Zone 9	Zone 10
Apple	hardy varieties	X	X	X	low chill	low chill	low chill	*needs protection & low chill	X	low chill	hardy varieties
Apricot		hardy varieties	X	X	X		low chill	*needs protection & low chill	X	low chill	hardy varieties
Avocado				*needs protection		X	*needs protection				
Blackberry	hardy varieties	X	X	X	X	X	X	X	X	X	X
Blueberry	hardy varieties	X	X								
Cherry		X	X	X	X			X	X		X
Citrus				*needs protection	*needs protection		X	*needs protection	*needs protection	*needs protection	
Fig			X	X	X	X	X	X		X	
Grape		American varieties	X	X	X	X	X	X	X	X	
Olive			*needs protection	X	variable crop	variable crop	X	X		X	
Peach		hardy varieties	X	X	low chill	low chill	low chill	*needs protection & low chill	X	low chill	hardy varieties
Pear			X	variable crop	low chill	low chill	low chill	*needs protection & low chill	X	low chill	hardy varieties
Pecan				X			X	X		X	
Pistachio				X			X		X	X	X
Plum		X	X	X	low chill	low chill	X	Oriental best		Oriental best	X
Pomegranate			X	X	X	X	X	X	X	X	
Raspberry		X		X	X		X				
Strawberry	X	X	X	X	X	X	X	X	X	X	X
Walnut			X	X	X	X	X				

* needs protection from cold, heat, or wind   X = Zones in which plants will grow well

Strawberry

Avocado

Zinfandel grape

Blackberry

Dwarf peach

Right and left: *Catharanthus roseus* (Madagascar periwinkle)
Center: *Nierembergia solanaceae* (cupflower)

Arctotis hybrid (African daisy)

ANNUALS

Botanical Name / Common Name	Adaptation	Description	Culture
Amaranthus tricolor Joseph's coat	All zones	1½ to 5 feet tall. Grown for vivid multicolored foliage in reds, greens, and golds. Tropical looking.	Best in dry infertile soil in hot sunny location.
Arctotis hybrids African daisy	Zones 3–6	1-foot-tall spreading mound of gray-green foliage. Brightly colored 3-inch daisylike flowers bloom in spring and summer. Color depends on cultivar. Good border plant.	Very tolerant of drought, heat, wind, salt air, and soil. Full sun. Lives over as a perennial in warm climates.
Calendula officinalis Calendula	All zones	Dense clump to 2 feet tall. Long narrow aromatic leaves and 3-inch daisylike orange, yellow, or cream flowers. Good bedding plant.	Tolerant of drought and heat. Full sun. Plant in fall for late fall to spring bloom in mild climates and spring to summer bloom in colder climates.
Catharanthus roseus (*Vinca rosea*) Madagascar periwinkle	All zones	Perennial grown as annual, to 18 inches tall. Glossy deep green leaves. Pink, mauve, or white phloxlike flowers bloom summer into fall. Dwarf and creeping cultivars. Good ground cover or bedding plant.	Tolerant of drought but best with some water. Also tolerates heat and air pollution. Resistant to insects. Full sun, part shade. Plant in late spring. Self-sows.
Centaurea cyanus Cornflower, bachelor's-button	All zones	Summer annual 1 to 3 feet tall. Usually blue (sometimes violet, red, pink, or white) frilled flowers. Recommended blue cultivars: 'Blue Diamond', 2 feet tall; 'Jubilee Gems', 1 foot tall. Good cut flowers.	Tolerant of drought, heat, wind, and salt air. Full sun. Sow seeds in early spring.
Convolvulus tricolor Dwarf morningglory	All zones	Prostrate compact summer annual forming neat 1-foot-tall mound covered with blue, lavender, or pink flowers. Good in rock gardens.	Blooms best when kept on dry side. Needs full sun and heat. Sow seeds in early spring.
Coreopsis tinctoria Calliopsis	All zones	6 inches to 3 feet tall. Smooth leaves, wispy stems. Yellow, bronze, red, or bicolored flowers resembling sunflowers bloom all summer. Dwarf cultivars available. Good in borders and as cut flowers.	Tolerant of drought, heat, and soil. Sow seeds in early spring. Reseeds freely.
Cosmos bipinnatus Cosmos	All zones	Open sprawling summer annual 3 to 6 feet tall. Lacy bright green foliage and daisylike magenta, white, pink, or lavender flowers bloom summer to fall. Good cut flowers.	Very tolerant of drought, heat, and salt air. Sow seeds in early spring. Reseeds freely.

Centaurea cyanus (cornflower)

Cosmos bipinnatus (cosmos)

ANNUALS

Botanical Name Common Name	Adaptation	Description	Culture
Dimorphotheca sinuata Cape marigold	All zones	To 12 inches tall with narrow sparsely toothed leaves and daisylike flowers in white, orange-yellow, salmon, or rose. Good in masses.	Looks good without irrigation. Best in hot sunny climates. Excellent choice for winter-spring color in zones 7–10. Plant in fall in warm climates, spring in cooler areas.
Eschscholzia californica California poppy	All zones	Perennial usually grown as an annual. 12 to 15 inches tall. Gray-green ferny foliage, pale yellow to deep orange large buttercuplike flowers. Cultivars with single or double scarlet, salmon, rose, or white flowers. Good for natural gardens.	Looks good without irrigation. Tolerant of heat, wind, salt air, and soil. Full sun. Sow seeds in fall in mild-winter climates and spring elsewhere. Blooms 4 to 5 weeks from seed. Doesn't transplant well.
Euphorbia marginata Snow-on-the-mountain	All zones	Summer annual to 2 feet tall. Grown for attractive fleshy gray-green leaves with white margins. Good in masses and borders. Milky white juice can irritate the skin.	Very tolerant of drought, heat, and soil. Extremely easy to grow. Sow seeds in early spring. May self-sow invasively if not checked.
Gomphrena globosa Globe amaranth	All zones	Stiffly branched plant 10 to 30 inches tall. Oval green leaves 3 inches long. 1-inch round papery lavender, white, or pink flowers last indefinitely in dried arrangements.	Tolerant of drought, heat, and wind.
Lobularia maritima Sweet alyssum	All zones	3- to 6-inch trailing mounds of green foliage covered with small fragrant flowers most of the year. 'Carpet of Snow', white; 'Rosie O'Day', deep rose; 'Royal Carpet', violet. Good border or bulb cover.	Very tolerant of drought—looks good without irrigation. Also tolerates heat, wind, salt air, and soil. Summer annual in zones 1–4, carries over as a perennial elsewhere.
Mirabilis jalapa Four-o'clock	All zones	Perennial grown as annual in cold climates. Rounded, shrublike to 3 feet tall. Attractive dark green foliage. Trumpet-shaped white, yellow, red, pink, or bicolored flowers bloom midsummer through fall. Sometimes several colors appear on same plant. Blossoms open in late afternoon to exude fragrance. Natural garden.	Very tolerant of drought, heat, wind, air pollution, salt air, and soil. Easy to grow. Sow seeds in early spring. Reseeds in warm climates. In cold climates roots can be dug up, stored in a cool dry place over winter, and replanted in spring.

Eschscholzia californica (California poppy)

Sanvitalia 'Mandarin orange' (creeping zinnia)

Gomphrena globosa (globe amaranth)

ANNUALS

Botanical Name Common Name	Adaptation	Description	Culture
Myosotis sylvatica Forget-me-not	All zones	Low-spreading plant 6 inches to 1 foot tall. Green hairy leaves. Profusion of pale blue flowers with yellow centers. Good in natural gardens and as a bulb cover.	Very tolerant of drought, heat, wind, salt air, and soil. Prefers part shade, but tolerates full sun. Sow seeds in spring or early summer for fall bloom, in early fall for spring bloom. Reseeds freely.
Portulaca grandiflora Rose moss	All zones	Succulent trailing summer annual 6 inches tall and 18 inches wide. Fleshy pointed leaves and reddish stems. Roselike flowers open only in sun from early spring to frost. Many vivid colors; usually sold mixed. Some specialty seed companies sell single colors. Good in rock gardens.	Very tolerant of drought and intense heat. Full sun, rocky or sandy soil. Sow seeds in early spring. Reseeds freely.
Sanvitalia procumbens Creeping zinnia	All zones	Trailing summer annual to 6 inches tall and 1½ feet wide. Resembles miniature zinnia. Yellow or orange flowers with purple centers bloom from summer to frost. Good in rock gardens or as a dense ground cover.	Very tolerant of drought and heat. Full sun, good drainage. Sow seeds in early spring. Don't cover the seeds—they need light to germinate.
Tithonia rotundifolia Mexican sunflower	All zones	Perennial grown as summer annual, to 6 feet tall. Large velvety leaves on erect stems. Brilliant red-orange flowers with yellow centers resembling single dahlias bloom summer to frost. Good for cut flowers or background plant.	Tolerant of drought and heat. Full sun. Does well in the desert. Sow seeds in late spring.

Aurinia saxatilis (basket-of-gold)

Achillea filipendulina (fernleaf yarrow)

Armeria maritima (sea pink)

PERENNIALS

Botanical Name Common Name	Adaptation	Description	Culture
Achillea filipendulina Fernleaf yarrow	All zones	Open, erect to 4 feet tall. Ferny, soft-textured green foliage. Broad flat-topped clusters of tiny yellow flowers bloom in summer. Good for fresh or dried arrangements.	Very tolerant of drought, heat, and soil. Full sun. Divide every 3 to 4 years.
Anthemis tinctoria Golden marguerite	All zones	2-foot bushy clump with masses of small golden daisies in summer. Fernlike leaves are dark green above, white and woolly below. Aromatic when bruised. Short-lived but useful in borders and as cut flowers.	Tolerant of drought, heat, and soil. Full sun. Divide every other year.
Armeria maritima Sea pink	All zones	Dense cushion of grasslike foliage 3 to 4 inches tall. Long-stemmed small pinkish flowers bloom in late spring and sporadically throughout year in mild climates. Good rock garden plant.	Best in dry, infertile soil and full sun. Tolerates heat, wind, and salt air. Divide clump after 4 years or so.
Asclepias tuberosa Butterfly weed	All zones	18 to 36 inches tall. Lance-shaped dark green leaves. Brilliant orange-red flower clusters in summer attract butterflies, hummingbirds, bees. Fruit is attractive in dried arrangements.	Long taproot makes plant drought tolerant and hard to transplant or divide. Best in light, sandy, infertile soil and full sun. Tolerates wind.
Aspidistra elatior Cast-iron plant	Zones 3–7, 9	Tropical-looking foliage plant. Dark green arching leaves 4 inches wide and to 2½ feet long. Clump gradually grows in diameter. Good plant in deep shade.	Very tolerant of drought, heat, wind, salt air, and soil. Full shade in zones 7 and 9. Can take part shade elsewhere.
Aurinia saxatilis Basket-of-gold	All zones	Low and bushy to 1 foot tall. Dense gray-green foliage. Tiny yellow flowers cover plant in spring. Short-lived. Good in rock gardens.	Tolerates drought, heat, wind, and soil. Full sun, good drainage.
Baptisia australis False-indigo	All zones	Shrubby rounded mass 3 to 6 feet tall and wide. Cloverlike bright green leaves. Spikes of showy pea-shaped lavender flowers appear in late spring. Good in masses.	Long taproot makes plant drought tolerant and hard to divide. Grow from plants—may not flower for years when grown from seed. Best in well-drained infertile soil and full sun.

Erigeron karvinskianus (fleabane)

Hemerocallis species (daylily)

PERENNIALS

Botanical Name Common Name	Adaptation	Description	Culture
Belamcanda chinensis Blackberry lily	All zones	Clump of sword-shaped irislike foliage to 3 feet tall. Star-shaped orange flowers with red dots appear above foliage in late summer. Ornamental seed clusters resembling blackberries used in dried arrangements.	Tolerant of drought. Full sun, good drainage. Divide rhizome for more plants.
Centaurea cineraria Dusty-miller	Zones 4–10	Dense clump to 18 inches tall. Grown for velvety, white-lobed leaves and not for 1-inch purple or yellow flowers bloom in summer. Good border plant and for color contrast.	Best in dry soil and full sun. Tolerates heat and wind.
Ceratostigma plumbaginoides Dwarf plumbago	Zones 2–6	Trailing semievergreen mat to 1 foot tall. 2-inch green leaves turn bronzy in cool weather. Wiry reddish stems. Intense blue flowers bloom in summer and fall. Good in rock gardens.	More tolerant of drought in part shade. Also tolerates heat and soil. Divide every 4 years or so.
Dietes vegeta Fortnight lily	Zones 4–7	Clump of narrow, stiff irislike leaves to 4 feet tall. Small white irises with orange and brown blotches in the center bloom most of the year. Good accent plant or around pools.	Very tolerant of drought, heat, wind, salt air, and soil. Full sun or light shade. Don't remove entire flower stems—they produce flowers for many years. Cut back above a leaf joint near base of plant.
Erigeron karvinskianus Fleabane	Zones 4–7, 9	Prostrate, trailing plant to 2 feet tall. Profusion of small pinkish white daisylike flowers with yellow centers bloom most of the year. Good in rock gardens and borders.	Does very well with no water—even in dry rock walls. Can become invasive if not kept in check. Cut to ground yearly to renew. Tolerates heat, wind, salt air, and soil. Full sun, part shade.
Gaillardia × *grandiflora* Blanketflower	All zones	To 4 feet tall. Short-lived. Gray-green foliage. Large daisylike flowers with yellow and orange or red petals and maroon centers bloom late spring to fall. 'Goblin', 1 foot tall. Good in borders.	Very tolerant of drought and heat. Full sun. Easy to grow from seed, flowers the first year. Divide annually.
Helianthemum nummularium Sunrose	All zones	Spreading, trailing mat to 1 foot tall. Green or grayish leaves with fuzzy undersides. Color of showy 1-inch spring flowers depends on cultivar.	Tolerant of drought, heat, salt air, and soil. Full sun, good drainage. Shear after flowering to encourage fall bloom.

Gaillardia × grandiflora (blanketflower)

PERENNIALS

Botanical Name Common Name	Adaptation	Description	Culture
Hemerocallis hybrids Daylily	All zones	Clump of bright green evergreen or deciduous strap-shaped leaves with clusters of large flowers on stiff stems. Depending on cultivar, may grow 1 to 6 feet tall including flowers. Many colors, some fragrant. Exceptionally long-lived. Good near pools or as an accent.	Tough plant. Very tolerant of drought, salt air, and soil. Full sun or part shade in hottest areas. Divide clump for more plants—usually not necessary otherwise.
Liatris spicata Gayfeather	Zones 1–6	Vertical accent usually to 3 feet tall. Rose, lavender, or purple flower spikes in summer. Flowers open over time from top of spike to bottom. Dark green grassy leaves up to 16 inches long on flower stalk.	Tolerant of drought but best with occasional water. Also tolerates heat, cold, and soil. Full sun, part shade.
Limonium perezii Sea lavender	Zones 5, 7	Rounded clump of rich green leaves to 4 inches wide and 1 foot long. Stems to 3 feet long bear broad clusters of tiny purple flowers with white centers late spring to fall. Good for dried arrangements.	Very tolerant of drought—looks good with no irrigation. Also tolerates heat, wind, salt air, and soil. Full sun, part shade.
Lobelia laxiflora Lobelia	Zones 3–7, 9	Spreading mat to 2 feet tall. Narrow leaves on upright stems. Tubular honeysuckle-like orange-red flower spikes bloom in spring and summer. Good in borders.	Very tolerant of drought and heat. Full sun, part shade. Survives with considerable neglect.
Nierembergia hippomanica var. *violacea* Dwarf cupflower	Zones 4–9	6- to 12-inch mound with small dark green leaves. Violet cup-shaped flowers all summer. 'Purple Robe' recommended. Good border plant.	Tolerant of drought and heat. Full sun. Part shade in desert. Cut back after flowering to encourage new growth.
Oenothera berlandieri Mexican evening primrose	All zones	Low-spreading mat. Showy summer display of 1½-inch pink flowers held on upright stems 1 foot tall.	Very tolerant of drought, heat, and wind. Full sun. Can become invasive if not checked.

Upper left: *Romneya coulteri* (matilija-poppy)

Penstemon heterophyllus (penstemon, beardtongue)

Stachys byzantina (lamb's-ears)

Oenothera berlandieri (Mexican evening primrose)

PERENNIALS

Botanical Name Common Name	Adaptation	Description	Culture
Penstemon heterophyllus var. *purdyi* Penstemon, beardtongue	Zones 3–10	Clump 1 to 2 feet tall. Narrow dark green leaves. Spikes of tubular lavender to blue flowers bloom in spring and summer. 'Blue Bedder' common cultivar. Short-lived.	Best in infertile, well-drained soil with infrequent water. Tolerates heat and wind. Full sun. Part shade in desert.
Romneya coulteri Matilija-poppy	All zones	Spectacular plant 3 to 8 feet tall. Gray-green lobed leaves. Crepe paper–like white flowers with golden centers, to 9 inches across, appear in spring and summer.	Very tolerant of drought, heat, wind, and soil. Full sun. Invasive—withhold summer water to check growth. Cut to ground each fall. Good erosion control plant.
Stachys byzantina Lamb's-ears	All zones	Prostrate spreading mat 12 to 18 inches tall. Grown for silvery white, soft, woolly, tongue-shaped leaves. Rosy flower stalks appear in summer. Good in borders and for color contrast.	Very tolerant of drought, heat, wind, and salt air. Full sun, part shade. Cut back yearly in early spring to renew growth. Divide every 4 years.
Teucrium chamaedrys Germander	All zones	Low woody mound to 1 foot tall. Dark green toothed leaves. Reddish purple or white flowers bloom in summer. Good edging plant.	Tolerant of drought, heat, and wind. Prune back in early spring to force branching.

Kniphofia uvaria (red-hot-poker)

Festuca ovina var. glauca (blue fescue)

Pennisetum setaceum (fountaingrass)

GRASSES AND GRASSY PLANTS

Botanical Name Common Name	Adaptation	Description	Culture
Festuca ovina var. *glauca* Blue fescue	All zones	Mounding grass 6 to 10 inches high. Leaves are blue-green and fine textured. Use as a small accent or undulating ground cover.	Drought tolerant except in zones 7–10 where it requires regular water. Full sun. Shear near the ground after flowers bloom.
Kniphofia uvaria Red-hot-poker	Zones 1–6	Member of the lily family with coarse-looking grassy leaves 2 to 4 feet long. Bright red, orange, or yellow flower spikes appear in spring and summer. Use in background masses.	Tolerant of drought, heat, and wind. Full sun, part shade.
Miscanthus sinensis Maiden grass	All zones	Graceful perennial grass growing to 6 feet tall. 'Gracillimus' has lacy beige flowers that can be cut and dried. 'Variegatus' leaves have green and white stripes. 'Zebrinus' has yellow stripes.	Tolerant of drought and soil. Full sun, part shade. Cut back before new growth starts in spring.
Nolina microcarpa Beargrass	Zones 3–10	Not an actual grass, but has a grassy appearance. Member of the agave family, growing to 18 inches. Flowers on stems above the leaves bloom in summer. Seed husks are ornamental and remain on the plant through fall.	Very tolerant of drought and tough conditions. Full sun.
Pennisetum setaceum Fountaingrass	All zones	Grassy clump to 3 feet tall and wide. Long, narrow, bright green foliage. Soft, almost tropical seed plumes appear in masses above leaves in late summer. 'Cupreum' has darker leaves and reddish brown plumes. Excellent with rocks and for streambed effect. Dormant in winter.	Very tolerant of drought and soil. Full sun. Cut back before seeds form on flower spikes or plant can become invasive. Use cut flowers in arrangements.
Phalaris arundinacea Ribbon grass	All zones	Spreading clump to 3 feet tall. 6- to 12-inch leaves have white stripes. Top growth browns in fall but remains erect. Handsome as a perennial border or backdrop for other plants.	Very tolerant of drought, heat, cold, and soil. Full sun, part shade. Invasive—plant only in confined areas, such as a section of concrete or clay drainpipe, to prevent runners from spreading.

Arctostaphylos species (manzanita)

Delosperma species (ice plant)

GROUND COVERS

Botanical Name Common Name	Adaptation	Description	Culture
Acacia redolens Prostrate acacia	Zones 5-7, 9	Fast growing to 2 feet tall, spreading 10 to 12 feet. Long, narrow gray-green leaves. Bright yellow flowers in spring.	Tolerant of drought, heat, and soil. Full sun. Remove upright growth to maintain ground-cover effect. Excellent bank cover.
Achillea tomentosa Woolly yarrow	All zones	Low-spreading mat to 10 inches tall. Gray-green fernlike foliage. Flat-topped yellow flower clusters bloom in spring and summer. Often used in rock gardens.	Tolerant of drought, heat, and soil. Full sun, part shade. Can be used as low-traffic lawn substitute if flowers are removed by mowing.
Antennaria rosea Pink-pussytoes	All zones	Gray-green leaves form a tight mat a few inches tall and spreading to 2 feet. White to pink flowers form in clusters above leaves in spring.	Drought tolerant. Accepts sun or filtered shade. Excellent on rocky slopes.
Arctostaphylos species and cultivars Manzanita	Zones 3–6	Slow-growing ground covers with glossy green leaves and tiny white bell-shaped flowers in spring. 'Emerald Carpet' is the greenest, most uniform, and most drought tolerant of the low-growing manzanitas. 'Point Reyes', 'Wayside', and 'Monterey Carpet' are also widely used.	Tolerant of drought and sun on the coast. Needs afternoon shade and water every 2 to 3 weeks in hotter areas.
Artemisia species Artemisia, dusty-miller	All zones	Slow-growing ground cover from a few inches to 2 feet tall, spreading to 2 feet. All have lacy, silver gray, finely cut foliage. *A. caucasica* 'Silver Spreader' is very low growing. *A. schmidtiana* 'Silver Mound' forms a dense mound.	Tolerates drought and heat. Full sun, good drainage.
Baccharis pilularis Coyotebrush	Zones 3–6, 8, 10,	Mounding to 2 feet tall, spreading to 6 feet. Small round dark green leaves. Neat appearance. 'Twin Peaks' and 'Pigeon Point' are improved male forms. 'Centennial', a hybrid between *B. pilularis* and *B. sarothroides*, is an excellent desert variety.	Tolerant of drought and heat. Full sun, part shade. Excellent low-maintenance ground cover. Prune back to renew.
Cerastium tomentosum Snow-in-summer	All zones	Fast growing to 4 to 6 inches tall, forming a dense mat 2 feet wide in one year. Silver gray leaves. Small white flowers bloom late spring through summer.	Drought tolerant. Best in full sun and and well-drained soil. Aggressive spreader.
Coprosma × *kirkii* Coprosma	Zones 4–5	Tough ground cover 2 to 3 feet tall and spreading. Small olive green leaves, twiggy habit.	Tolerant of drought, heat, wind, and salt air. Good erosion-control plant. Prune to keep dense.

Hypericum calycinum (St.-Johnswort)

Juniperus chinensis var. *procumbens* (juniper)
Center: *Portulaca grandiflora* (rose moss)

GROUND COVERS

Botanical Name Common Name	Adaptation	Description	Culture
Cotoneaster species Cotoneaster	Zones 1–6, 8, 10 *C. horizontalis* All zones *C. dammeri*	Range of sizes from less than 1 foot to tall shrubs. Small gray-green leaves. Pink to white flowers bloom in spring followed by bright red berries in fall. *C. horizontalis*, rock cotoneaster, deciduous for short time, to 3 feet tall and 15 feet wide. *C. dammeri*, bearberry cotoneaster, to 6 inches tall, branches root freely.	Drought tolerant. Plant on dry slope to control erosion. Thrives on little or no maintenance. Full sun. Part shade in desert.
Dalea greggii Trailing indigo bush	Zones 7, 9	Low, mounding, mat-forming plant spreading to 4 feet or more. Very small gray-green leaves form on long stems. Tiny purplish flowers bloom spring to summer.	Tolerant of drought, heat, cold to 15° F, and soil. Excellent low cover for southwest deserts.
Delosperma nubigenum Ice plant	All zones	Very low, mat-forming, spreading to several feet. Succulent light green foliage, yellow flowers. 'Alpha' has white flowers. Blooms throughout the year. Hardiest of all ice plants. Other ice plant genera include *Carpobrotus, Drosanthemum, Lampranthus,* and *Maleophora.*	Tolerant to drought and cold to -25° F. Full sun, good drainage.
Gazania species Gazania	Zones 4–10	Fast-growing mat 6 to 12 inches tall. Two forms: trailing (*G. rigens* var. *leucolaena*) and clumping (*G. rigens*). Trailing varieties spread rapidly. Many flower colors available in both forms.	Thrives in heat and full sun. Divide trailing varieties every 3 to 4 years. Tolerant of drought but looks better with occasional water.
Hypericum calycinum St.-Johnswort	Zones 2–10	Prostrate spreading mat 1 foot tall. It roots where branches touch the soil. Partly deciduous in cold-winter climates. Leaves are green in sun, yellowish in shade. 2-inch bright yellow flowers bloom in summer and sporadically throughout the year.	Very tolerant of drought, heat, wind, and soil. Full sun. Good erosion-control plant. Can become invasive if not checked.
Juniperus species Juniper	All zones	Extremely broad range of low-maintenance plants from ground covers to 50-foot trees. *J. horizontalis* cultivars include 'Bar Harbor', 'Blue Chip', 'Hughes', 'Webberi', and 'Wiltonii'. *J. sabina* cultivars include 'Buffalo' and 'Tamariscifolia'. *J. chinensis* var. *procumbens* 'Nana' has prickly foilage. Prostrate junipers make good rock-garden plants.	Tolerant of drought and soil. Provide afternoon shade and occasional water in hottest climates.

Lower right: *Rosmarinus officinalis* 'Prostratus' (dwarf or prostrate rosemary)
Center: *Lavandula angustifolia* (English lavender)

Lantana montevidensis (lantana)

Santolina species (lavender cotton)

GROUND COVERS

Botanical Name Common Name	Adaptation	Description	Culture
Lantana species Lantana	Zones 5-9	*L. montevidensis* has arching branches 1 to 2 feet tall, spreading 3 to 6 feet. Leaves are small, coarse, and gray-green. Purple flowers in small clusters are profuse throughout long growing season. *L. camara* is larger, to 3 feet tall, with bright multicolored flowers in yellow, orange, and red.	Tolerant of drought, reflected heat, and soil. Full sun. An annual in cold-winter regions. Prune back in spring. Good erosion-control plant.
Mahonia repens Creeping mahonia	All zones	Grows 12 to 18 inches tall in sun, taller in shade, with equal spread. Bluish green hollylike leaves turn bronzy in winter. Yellow flowers bloom in spring, followed by dark blue berries that attract birds.	Tolerant of drought. Full sun, part shade. Good plant for attracting birds and for controlling erosion on slopes.
Osteospermum fruticosum Trailing African daisy	Zones 4-6	Fast growing to 1 foot tall and spreading as much as 4 feet in one year. 2-inch daisylike white or deep purple flowers bloom late fall through winter. Excellent rock-garden plant.	Tolerates drought but best with some water in hottest climates. Full sun.
Phlox subulata Moss pink	Zones 1-5a	Colorful mat 4 to 6 inches tall spreading about twice as wide. Needle-shaped olive green leaves look like moss. Lavender, blue, pink, or white star-shaped flowers appear late spring through summer.	Fair drought tolerance after plants are established. Full sun. Tolerates cold to -40° F.
Phyla nodiflora Lippia	Zones 4-10	Low prostrate tough ground cover or lawn substitute. Small grayish green leaves. Tiny pink flower spikes bloom during warm weather. Dormant in winter.	Very tolerant of drought in coastal areas. Needs regular water in very hot climates. Doesn't need mowing—but can be mowed to remove the flower heads, which attract bees. Full sun.

Left: *Verbena* species

Zauschneria californica (California fuchsia)

Thymus pseudolanuginosus (woolly thyme)

GROUND COVERS

Botanical Name Common Name	Adaptation	Description	Culture
Rosmarinus officinalis 'Prostratus' Dwarf or prostrate rosemary	Zones 3–10	Dense covering to about 2 feet tall, spreading 4 to 6 feet. Aromatic leaves are dark green above and gray-green below. Blue flowers in spring are favorites of bees. 'Lockwood de Forest' has bluer flowers. Makes an excellent cascade over walls.	Needs occasional water in desert—thrives with no water elsewhere. Tolerates heat and soil. Full sun, good drainage. Controls erosion on slopes.
Santolina species Lavender cotton	All zones	Mounding form to 2 feet tall, spreading 2 to 3 feet. Yellow buttonlike flowers in summer. Aromatic foliage. *S. chamaecyparissus* has silver gray leaves and *S. virens* dark green leaves.	Very drought tolerant in cooler regions. May need regular water in hotter areas. Full sun. Prune to keep low. May die to ground yearly in cold climates.
Thymus species Thyme	All zones	Woolly thyme, *T. pseudolanuginosus,* forms a gray-green mat a few inches high and has tiny pink flowers. Creeping thyme, *T. praecox,* forms a 4-inch green mat and has purple flowers. Aromatic foliage.	Drought tolerant in cooler areas. Needs regular water in hottest climates. Full sun, good drainage.
Verbena species Verbena	Zones 4–10 *V. peruviana* All zones *V. gooddingii* *V. rigida*	*V. peruviana* (also sold as *V. chamaedryfolia*) grows to 8 inches tall and spreads fast to 2 feet or more. Small red, pink, lavender, purple, or white flowers. *V. gooddingii* has purplish pink flowers and reseeds. *V. rigida* is more drought tolerant than Peruvian verbena.	Tolerant of drought. Thrives on heat and sun. Hardy to 25° F. Grown as annuals in cold-winter climates.
Zauschneria californica California fuchsia, Hummingbird flower	Zones 5–6	Fast growing to 2 feet tall, spreading 3 to 4 feet. Leaves are gray-green. Bright red or white tubular flowers bloom in late summer. *Z. cana* is similar but more mounding in form.	Tolerates drought and heat. Best grown in informal gardens or on hillsides. Tends to get rangy and become invasive.

Top: Bougainvillea; bottom: Yucca

Lonicera japonica (Japanese honeysuckle)

Rosa banksiae (Lady Banks rose)

VINES

Botanical Name Common Name	Adaptation	Description	Culture
Antigon leptopus Queen's wreath	Zones 5b–7, 9	Deciduous vine (evergreen in warmest winter climates), fast growing to 40 feet or more. Large heart-shaped leaves and red to pink or sometimes white flowers. 'Baja Red' is red-blooming variety. 'Album', white variety, is harder to find. Plant is tender and dies to ground in cold, coming back next spring. Needs support.	Can grow without irrigation in zone 7, but may die to the ground in summer—will come back in spring. Needs regular water elsewhere. Thrives in sun and heat.
Bougainvillea species Bougainvillea	Zones 5–7, 9	Shrubby mounding deciduous vine grown for dazzling color of bracts (modified leaves surrounding tiny flowers). Cultivars available in red, purple, orange, white, and other colors. Green heart-shaped leaves.	Very tolerant of drought, heat, and salt air. Full sun. Prune heavily to renew growth. Plant without removing container because of extremely sensitive roots. Cut bottom of can or poke holes in sides. Plant may take 2 years to establish itself and require frequent irrigation during that time. Once established, roots are no longer sensitive and plants become extremely drought tolerant.
Clytostoma callistegioides Lavender trumpet vine	Zones 5–7	Evergreen vine, to 35 feet. Climbs by tendrils, needs support. Glossy green leaflets. 3-inch trumpet-shaped lavender flowers in spring.	Occasional deep irrigation. Tolerates heat. Full sun, part shade.
Distictis buccinatoria Blood-red trumpet vine	Zones 4–6	Evergreen vine, slow at first and then fast growing to 30 feet. Climbs by tendrils and suction disks. Medium green leaflets. 2- to 3-inch trumpet-shaped orange-red flowers bloom during hot spells.	Tolerant of drought, heat, wind, and salt air. Full sun. Prune yearly to keep from becoming rampant. Suction disks can mar wood and painted surfaces.
Gelsemium sempervirens Carolina jessamine	Zones 4–10	Shrubby evergreen vine, to 20 feet or more. Glossy green leaves. Fragrant yellow trumpet-shaped flowers late winter and early spring. Needs support. Can be allowed to sprawl as a ground cover.	Moderately drought tolerant—best with some water. Full sun. Prune heavily if vine gets top-heavy. All plant parts are poisonous.
Lonicera japonica Japanese honeysuckle	Zones 2–10	Evergreen (partly or completely deciduous in coldest areas), rampant growth to 30 feet or more. Fragrant flowers in spring and summer. 'Halliana', most commonly grown, has white flowers that turn pale yellow. Needs support. Can be allowed to sprawl as ground cover.	Tolerant of drought, soil, and poor drainage. Prune severely in late winter to renew growth and to control rampant habit.

Wisteria species

Vitis species (grape vine)

VINES

Botanical Name Common Name	Adaptation	Description	Culture
Macfadyena unguis-cati Cat's-claw vine Yellow trumpet vine	Zones 4–10	Partly deciduous vine, fast growing to 40 feet. Small leaves create fine texture. Slender stems and tendrils cling to most surfaces to cover large areas quickly. Yellow trumpet-shaped flowers are profuse in spring.	Tolerant of drought and heat. Full sun. Prune severely after bloom. Can mar wood and painted surfaces.
Polygonum aubertii Silver-lace vine	All zones	Evergreen to deciduous, rampant growth to 20 feet. Glossy green heart-shaped leaves. Small creamy flowers in billowy masses appear spring to fall. Needs support.	Very drought tolerant in cooler climates. Deep irrigation once a month elsewhere. Tolerates heat, wind, and soil. Prune severely in late winter to control growth.
Rosa banksiae Lady Banks rose	Zones 3–10	Evergreen (deciduous in cold climates), climbing rose, fast growing to 20 feet. No prickles. 'Alba Plena', double white fragrant flowers; 'Lutea', double yellow unscented flowers. Needs support.	Drought tolerant. Resistant to almost all insects and diseases.
Solanum jasminoides Potato vine	Zones 4–7, 9	Evergreen (deciduous in cold winter areas), very fast growing to 30 feet. Climbs by twining, needs support. Clusters of 1-inch white flowers bloom most of the year. Creates light shade as arbor cover.	Tolerant of drought, heat, and wind. Full sun.
Tecomaria capensis Cape honeysuckle	Zones 5–7, 9	Evergreen, fast growing to 25 feet. Can be used as a ground cover or pruned hard as a 6-foot shrub. Rich green leaflets. Reddish orange tubular flowers bloom fall through winter.	Moderately drought tolerant but best with occasional water. Tolerates heat, wind, and salt air. Full sun, part shade.
Vitis species Grape	Zone depends on variety	Deciduous, fast growing. Can be used for arbor shade or trained for fruit production. Check locally for best wine or table grape variety.	Tolerant of drought and soil. Full sun for fruit production.
Wisteria species Wisteria	All zones	Deciduous, fast growing to 40 feet. Very heavy. Use strong support and tie stems. Large drooping clusters of white, pink, blue, or lavender flowers in spring. Grafted plants offer predictable flower color. Seedlings are unpredictable and may not bloom for years.	Tolerant of drought and heat. Full sun, part shade. Prune yearly to control growth.

Berberis thunbergii (barberry)

SHRUBS

Botanical Name Common Name	Adaptation	Description	Culture
Anisacanthus thurberi Desert honeysuckle	Zones 4, 6–10	Evergreen to deciduous, 3 to 5 feet tall. Light green leaves. 1½-inch tubular yellow flowers in spring and summer.	Tolerant of drought and soil. Full sun. Cut to ground every winter to promote denser growth. Good desert plant.
Arbutus unedo Strawberry-tree	Zones 3–10	Evergreen shrub or small tree. Usually around 8 feet tall but can grow to 25 feet. Small white flowers and edible but mealy strawberrylike fruit appear at same time in winter. 'Compacta' grows 6 to 8 feet tall.	Tolerant of drought, heat, wind, and salt air. Full sun, part shade.
Atriplex species Saltbush	Zones 2–10 *A. canescens* Zones 3–4, 6–10 *A. lentiformis* Zones 4–6 *A. l.* var. *breweri*	*A. canescens*, four-wing saltbush, evergreen, to 8 feet tall, spreading 6 to 8 feet. Silver gray leaves and inconspicuous flowers. Use for accent or hedge. *A. lentiformis*, quail bush, deciduous, to 13 feet tall and 10 feet wide. Silver gray leaves. Use as screen or barrier. *Breweri* is a superior variety and nearly evergreen.	Very drought tolerant. Accepts salty soils and rugged growing conditions. Controls erosion on slopes.
Berberis species Barberry	Zones 3–5a, 8, 10	Evergreen and deciduous shrubs to 10 feet tall with similar spread. Most have spiny foliage, yellow flowers in spring, and colorful berries. Foliage of many deciduous species turns bright red or orange in fall. *B.* × *mentorensis*, evergreen to -5° F, grows to 7 feet tall. *B. thunbergii* 'Atropurpurea', deciduous, to 6 feet tall, rich purple foliage spring through summer if planted in full sun. *B. darwinii*, evergreen, to 10 feet tall, arching branches and profuse blooming.	Tolerant of drought and tough conditions. Prune to maintain attractive form—neglected plants can become ratty-looking. Spiny-leaved forms make good barriers.
Caesalpinia species Bird-of-paradise	Zones 5a, 6–7, 9 *C. pulcherrima* *C. mexicana* Zones 4–5a, 6–10 *C. gilliesii*	*C. pulcherrima*, red bird-of-paradise, deciduous (evergreen in warmest climates), fernlike foliage, and red or orange flowers with long red stamens in summer. *C. gilliesii*, yellow bird-of-paradise, is similar but foliage is not as lush and flowers are a less showy yellow. *C. mexicana* is evergreen with yellow flowers blooming year around.	Occasional irrigation for best blooms. Thrives in full sun and heat. *C. pulcherrima* dies to the ground with frost but rebounds in spring. *C. gilliesii* is hardy to 10° F.

Ceanothus species (wild lilac)

Chrysothamnus nauseosus (rabbitbrush)

SHRUBS

Botanical Name Common Name	Adaptation	Description	Culture
Calliandra species Fairy-duster	Zones 5–10 *C. californica* Zones 3–7, 9 *C. tweedii*	Large group of showy evergreen shrubs, many with feathery leaves and brushlike flowers consisting of stamens. *B. californica*, Baja fairy-duster, 3 to 4 feet tall, pink to red flowers in spring. *C. tweedii,* Trinidad flame bush, 6 to 8 feet tall, crimson flowers late winter to fall. It is less cold tolerant than Baja fairy-duster.	Tolerant of drought and soil. Full sun. Frost tender, so plant in warm microclimate.
Callistemon citrinus Lemon bottlebrush	Zones 4–7, 9	Evergreen roundheaded shrub or small tree, fast growing to 25 feet tall. Pinkish copper new growth turns medium green. Bright red bottlebrush-shaped flowers bloom at different times of the year and attract hummingbirds.	Occasional deep irrigation. Tolerates heat, wind, soil, and salt air. Full sun.
Cassia artemisiodes Feathery cassia	Zones 4–7, 9	An attractive evergreen shrub to 5 feet tall and spreading to 4 feet. Leaves are gray-green and feathery. Bright yellow flowers bloom late winter into spring.	Tolerant of drought and soil. Prune lightly after flowering. Susceptible to Texas root rot.
Ceanothus species Ceanothus Wild lilac	Zones 3, 5–6	Primarily evergreen shrubs, ground covers, and small trees. Flower colors range from white to blue to deep violet. Spring blooming. Ceanothus is short-lived: around 10 years. Many species and cultivars. Some of the best are: *C.* 'Concha', to 7 feet tall and wide, dark blue flowers, tolerates summer water; *C.* 'Frosty Blue', to 9 feet tall and wide, white-frosted blue flowers; *C.* 'Julia Phelps', to 7 feet tall and wide, dark blue flowers; *C. thyrsiflorus,* to 20 feet tall by 30 feet wide, light to dark blue flowers, among the hardiest.	Do not water after plant is established or it may succumb to root rot. Full sun, part shade.
Cercis occidentalis Western redbud	Zones 2–10	Deciduous shrub or small tree, 6 to 18 feet tall and wide. Usually multitrunked. Magenta flowers in spring, bright green heart-shaped leaves and red bean pods in summer, yellow or red foliage in fall, and bare red-brown branches in winter. Flowers best in cold-winter areas.	Very drought tolerant—grows wild with no water. Full sun, part shade. Prune to shape.

Cistus incanus (rockrose)

Cowania mexicana (cliffrose)

SHRUBS

Botanical Name Common Name	Adaptation	Description	Culture
Cercocarpus species Mountain mahogany	All zones	*C. ledifolius,* curl-leaf mahogany, evergreen, 5 to 15 feet tall, spreading as wide. Small dark green leathery leaves. Flowers are not showy, but long-plumed seedheads are attractive in fall. *C. montanus,* mountain mahogany, deciduous, usually 6 feet tall and as wide. Seedheads similar to those of curl-leaf mahogony.	Very drought tolerant. Full sun, part shade.
Chrysothamnus nauseosus Rabbitbrush	All zones	Deciduous shrub to 7 feet tall. Narrow silvery blue leaves. Some subspecies have greenish to white stems. Brilliant yellow flowers bloom profusely summer to fall.	Tolerant of drought and tough conditions including saline soil. Prune in winter to encourage flowering.
Cistus species Rockrose	Zones 3–7, 9	Evergreen shrubs with showy flowers in spring to early summer. *C. × hybridus,* white rockrose, 2 to 5 feet tall and spreading 6 to 8 feet, fragrant leaves, 1½-inch white flowers with yellow centers; *C. ladanifer,* crimson-spot rockrose, 3 to 5 feet tall and wide, fragrant, white 3-inch flowers with crimson spot at base of each petal; *C. × purpureus,* orchid rockrose, to 4 feet tall and wide, 3-inch purplish flowers with red spot at base of each petal.	Needs no water after becoming established. Full sun. Tolerates poor soil, heat, salt air, and wind.
Cordia boissieri Texas olive	Zones 4–10	Can be small tree but best as shrub 6 to 10 feet tall. Evergreen but loses leaves in severe frost. Clusters of white flowers in spring and summer.	Adapted to desert heat and drought but best with water 2 or 3 times a month. Full sun, part shade.
Cotoneaster species Cotoneaster	Zones 3–10 *C. lacteus* All zones *C. divaricatus*	Many forms of evergreen and deciduous shrubs. Also see Ground Covers, page 80. *C. lacteus,* evergreen, arching habit to about 8 feet tall. Can be trained as a small tree. 2-inch dark green leaves with white undersides. White flowers bloom late spring to early summer. Showy red berry clusters in fall. *C. divaricatus,* deciduous, to 6 feet tall, spreading as wide. Small dark green leaves turn reddish in fall. Bright red berries in fall. Some species such as *C. franchetii* and *C. buxifolius* (also sold as *C. pannosus*) are invasive.	Very tolerant of drought and soil. Full sun. Afternoon shade in desert. Good erosion-control plant. Thin, don't shear, to control growth.

Lavandula angustifolia (English lavender)

SHRUBS

Botanical Name Common Name	Adaptation	Description	Culture
Cowania mexicana Cliffrose	Zones 1–2, 7–10	Evergreen shrub to 7 feet tall and wide. Small dark green leaves. Fragrant roselike white to yellow flowers in summer. Attractive plumelike, feathery fruit follows.	Occasional deep irrigation. Full sun. Prune to improve appearance.
Dalea spinosa Smoke tree	Zones 7–9	Deciduous large shrub or small tree usually to around 12 feet tall. Violet flowers in spring. After leaves drop, dense silver gray branches resemble clouds of smoke. Good plant for informal desert garden.	Tolerant of drought, heat, and soil.
Dodonaea viscosa Hopbush	Zones 3–7, 9	Evergreen shrub, useful as informal hedge or screen. Native Arizona green form grows 6 to 10 feet tall and is hardier than purple-leaf forms. 'Purpurea' and 'Saratoga' must be planted in full sun—their purple leaves will turn green in shade.	Tolerant of drought, heat, soil, wind, and salt air. Full sun.
Elaeagnus pungens Thorny elaeagnus Silverberry	Zones 3–10	Evergreen, 8 to 15 feet tall. Thorny leaves create an effective barrier. Fragrant white flowers in fall. Red berries in spring. Variegated forms are more attractive. 'Fruitlandii', dark green leaves with silver flecks; 'Maculata', gold-blotched leaves; 'Marginata', silvery white margins; and 'Variegata', yellowish margins.	Tolerant of drought, heat, wind, and salt air. Full sun, part shade.
Eriogonum fasciculatum California buckwheat	Zones 4–6	Evergreen rounded clump 2 to 3 feet tall and a little wider. Pinkish white, long-stemmed flowers cover plant spring to fall.	Very tolerant of drought—needs no supplemental water in coastal areas. May need occasional water inland. Prune to shape, beginning when plant is young. Useful for erosion control.
Fallugia paradoxa Apache-plume	Zones 2–10	Deciduous shrub, 3 to 6 feet tall and slightly wider. Upright, graceful arching stems and branches. Large white roselike flowers bloom in summer. Attractive seedheads with silky pink plumes.	Very tolerant of drought and heat. Good erosion-control plant.

Leptospermum species (tea-tree)

Nandina domestica (heavenly bamboo)

SHRUBS

Botanical Name / Common Name	Adaptation	Description	Culture
Feijoa sellowiana Pineapple guava	Zones 3–7, 9	Evergreen shrub or small tree to 18 feet tall and wide. Leaves are grayish green above and white below. Unusual white, purple, and red flowers with edible petals in spring. Edible fruit ripens about 6 months later. Grows best on California coast and in inland valleys.	Tolerant of drought but best with occasional deep irrigation. Also tolerates wind. Full sun. Easily pruned as a shrub, multitrunked tree, hedge, or espalier.
Forestiera neomexicana New Mexican privet	All zones	Deciduous shrub to 10 feet tall and wide. Foliage turns yellow in fall. Some plants produce black fruit in fall. Makes a good screen because of fast growth.	Drought tolerant but best with occasional water. Full sun.
Heteromeles arbutifolia Toyon Christmas berry	Zones 3–10	Dense evergreen shrub to 10 feet tall. Can grow into a 25-foot tree. Dark green leathery leaves. Showy white flowers in summer. Clusters of red berries in fall and winter.	Looks good with no water. Tolerates heat and poor soil. Prefers full sun or part shade. Susceptible to fire blight and thrips.
Lavandula angustifolia English lavender	Zones 3–10	Evergreen shrub to 4 feet tall and wide. Aromatic gray foliage, fragrant 2-foot-long flower spikes in summer. Used in perfume and sachets. 'Hidcote' and 'Munstead' are popular dwarf cultivars to 1½ feet tall. Attracts bees.	Very tolerant of drought—looks good without supplemental irrigation. Full sun. Prune after bloom.
Leptospermum species Tea-tree	Zones 5–6	Evergreen shrubs or small trees. Tiny roselike flowers in spring. *L. laevigatum*, Australian tea-tree, 15 to 30 feet tall and wide, single white flowers, twisted trunk on old plants. Dwarf cultivars: 'Compactum' to 8 feet tall, 'Reevesii' to 4 feet tall. *L. scoparium* 'Ruby Glow', 6 to 8 feet tall and wide, double red flowers cover the entire plant in winter and spring.	Very tolerant of drought, heat, wind, and salt air. Does not tolerate alkaline soil. Full sun, good drainage. Do not prune into bare wood—will not resprout. Useful for erosion control.
Leucophyllum frutescens Texas ranger	Zones 3–10	Evergreen shrub, 5 to 10 feet tall. 'Compactum' is smaller and denser. Silvery foliage. Needs heat to produce violet flowers in summer.	Tolerant of drought, heat, and wind. Can be clipped into a hedge. Good desert plant.
Lysiloma thornberi Featherbush Fern-of-the-desert	Zones 5–7, 9–10	Evergreen to deciduous large shrub or small tree, to 15 feet tall. Feathery leaves give a subtropical effect. White to cream flowers cover branches in late spring. Good patio tree or background shrub.	Tolerant of drought and desert heat. Usually comes back if frost killed.

Pyracantha coccinea (firethorn)

Heteromeles arbutifolia (toyon, Christmas berry)

Nerium oleander (oleander)

SHRUBS

Botanical Name Common Name	Adaptation	Description	Culture
Nandina domestica Heavenly bamboo	Zones 3-10	Bamboolike, airy, upright evergreen shrub 5 to 8 feet tall and to 4 feet wide. Light green leaves turn reddish bronze in cool fall weather. Bright red berries follow. Attractive for close viewing.	Tolerates drought but best with moderate water. Needs shade in hottest areas. Can take sun elsewhere. Resistant to oak root fungus.
Nerium oleander Oleander	Zones 4-10	Popular evergreen shrub to 12 feet tall. Can be trained as a single or multitrunked tree. Leaves are narrow and dark green. Varieties with white, red, or pink flowers bloom from spring to fall. Dwarf varieties such as 'Petite' and 'Little Red' grow to less than 4 to 5 feet tall. Excellent casual hedge, screen, or windbreak.	Very tolerant of drought, heat, reflected light, wind, soil, and poor drainage. Best inland away from summer fog. Full sun. Does poorly in shade. All plant parts are poisonous.
Osmanthus species Osmanthus	Zones 3-6 *O. delavayi* Zones 4-7, 9 *O. fragrans* Zones 4-6, 10 *O. heterophyllus*	Evergreen shrubs or trees with fragrant, inconspicuous flowers. *O. delavayi*, 4 to 6 feet tall and wider with graceful arching branches; *O. fragrans*, 10 to 30 feet tall; *O. heterophyllus*, 4 to 6 feet tall, hollylike leaves.	Tolerant of drought and soil. Full sun, part shade; *O. delavayi* needs part shade in the desert.
Podocarpus macrophyllus Yew pine	Zones 3-7, 9	Slow-growing evergreen shrub or tree that can eventually reach 50 feet tall. Good espalier shrub. Narrow and upright with bright green leaves.	Tolerant of drought but best with occasional deep irrigation. Takes pruning well.
Prunus species	Zones 3-10 *P. caroliniana* Zones 3-7, 9 *P. ilicifolia* *P. lyonii* Zones 3-6 *P. lusitanica*	Evergreen forms include *P. caroliniana*, Carolina cherry-laurel; *P. ilicifolia*, hollyleaf cherry; *P. lusitanica*, Portugal laurel; and *P. lyonii*, Catalina cherry. All make excellent 10- to 20-foot screens or background plants.	Tolerant of drought. *P. caroliniana* is sensitive to alkaline and saline soils and does better in coastal California. All are resistant to oak root fungus.

SHRUBS

Botanical Name Common Name	Adaptation	Description	Culture
Punica granatum 'Nana' Dwarf pomegranate	Zones 3–10	Evergreen to deciduous shrubs to 3 feet tall. Reddish orange flowers in summer, followed by small dry red fruit.	Tolerant of drought, heat, and soil. Full sun.
Pyracantha coccinea Firethorn	All zones	Evergreen rounded shrub to 10 feet tall. Spiny green leaves, clusters of orange or red berries in fall. Many cultivars. Best firethorn for cold-winter areas; will do well in all but coldest parts of zone 1. Attracts birds.	Best in dry situations—will not tolerate excess water. Full sun. Susceptible to fireblight, scale, woolly aphids, and mites.
Raphiolepis indica Indian-hawthorn	Zones 3–7, 9–10	Evergreen, 3 to 5 feet tall and wide. Leaves are glossy, green, and leathery. Pink or white flowers bloom fall to spring. 'Springtime', 'Enchantress', and 'Ballerina' are improved cultivars.	Tolerant of drought, salt air, and soil. Full sun. Afternoon shade in desert.
Rhus species Sumac	Zones 3–10 *R. ovata* Zones 1–5a, 10 *R. glabra*	*R. ovata,* sugarbush, evergreen shrub, 3 to 10 feet tall. Glossy dark green leathery leaves. White to pink flowers in dense clusters in spring. Clusters of berries coated with sugar secretion appear summer to fall. Can be used to flavor drinks. More heat tolerant than *R. integrifolia,* lemonade berry, grown along the coast. *R. glabra* var. *cismontana,* smooth sumac, dwarf variety to 4 feet tall. Leaflets turn red in fall. Spreads by root suckers and can be invasive.	Very tolerant of drought, heat, and cold.
Ruellia peninsularis Ruellia	Zones 7, 9	Evergreen shrub to 3 feet tall. Profusion of purple flowers in summer and occasionally through the year. Can lose leaves in frost.	Needs ample water to become established but drought tolerant afterward.
Salvia species Sage	Zones 4–10 *S. greggii* Zones 5–10 *S. leucantha* *S. clevelandii*	Evergreen shrubs with fragrant foliage. *S. greggii,* autumn sage, bushy, to 4 feet tall, green foliage, red flowers bloom from spring to fall. *S. clevelandii,* blue sage, to 4 feet tall, gray-green foliage, blue flowers appear late spring to summer. *S. leucantha,* Mexican bush sage, to 4 feet tall, violet flower spikes summer to fall.	Drought tolerant, especially in coastal zones. Occasional water elsewhere. Full sun, part shade. Remove old flower stems of *S. leucantha* for more blooms.
Shepherdia argentea Silver buffaloberry	Zones 1–2, 10	Deciduous shrub usually around 6 feet tall. Silvery gray leaves. If pollinated, female plants produce sour berries used in jams. Attracts birds.	Tolerant of drought, cold, wind, and soil.
Simmondsia chinensis Jojoba	Zones 5b–10	Evergreen shrub, 4 to 8 feet tall and wide. Gray-green leathery leaves. Valued commercially for the oil from its acornlike seeds.	Drought tolerant but best with occasional water. Tolerates reflected heat. Full sun. Can be clipped into a hedge.
Sophora secundiflora Texas mountain laurel	Zones 4–10	Evergreen shrub or small tree, slow growing to 20 feet tall and 15 feet wide. Glossy green lobed leaves. Fragrant pea-shaped violet flowers hang from silvery branches in long clusters from late winter into spring. Long woody seedpods open to reveal poisonous red seeds.	Tolerant of sun, heat, and alkaline soil. Needs moderate water and good drainage. Grows better inland in zone 5a.
Xylosma congestum Shiny xylosma	Zones 4–10	Evergreen shrub usually growing 8 to 10 feet tall and as wide. Glossy yellow-green leaves give the plant a lush appearance. May drop leaves in a frost.	Drought tolerant but best with occasional deep irrigation. Also tolerates heat and soil. Full sun, part shade. Can be clipped into a hedge.

Upper right: *Acacia* species

Acer saccharinum (silver maple)

TREES

Botanical Name Common Name	Adaptation	Description	Culture
Acacia species Acacia	Zones 3–7 *A. baileyana* Zones 4–7, 9 *A. smallii*	Large group of evergreen and deciduous trees and large shrubs. Generally very fast growing and short-lived (some live only 20 years). Yellow flowers appear in winter or spring. *A. baileyana,* bailey acacia, evergreen, to 30 feet tall, feathery blue-gray foliage. *A. smallii,* sweet acacia, deciduous, to 25 feet tall, spiny branches. Many other species. All attract birds.	Very tolerant of drought—occasional deep irrigation in youth will encourage deep-rooted, stronger tree. Tolerates heat and soil. Full sun.
Acer saccharinum Silver maple	Zones 1–6	Deciduous roundheaded airy fast-growing tree, 40 to 100 feet tall. Bark and undersides of leaves are silver gray. Yellow to orange to red fall color.	Tolerates no irrigation or occasional waterings once established. Tolerates heat. Full sun, part shade.
Aesculus californica California buckeye	Zones 3, 5a, 6	Deciduous small tree, fast growing to 10 feet tall and then slower growing to 25 feet. Very wide spreading. 5 to 7 large leaflets per leaf. Fragrant pinkish white flowers in spring. Large inedible fruit, seeds poisonous unless treated with boiling water. Good shade tree.	Very tolerant of drought but drops its leaves in July without supplemental water. Retains leaves until fall if watered 2 or 3 times in summer. Tolerates heat and wind. Full sun, part shade. Good erosion-control tree.
Albizia julibrissin Silk tree	Zones 2–10	Deciduous, fast growing to 20 feet or more, with a broad canopy as wide or wider. Delicate fernlike leaves. Showy pink pincushion flowers in summer. Excellent small shade tree.	Drought tolerant but best with moderate water. Thrives in desert heat. Can be trained as single-trunked or multistemmed tree.
Alnus cordata Italian alder	Zones 3–9	Deciduous, to 35 feet tall. Pyramidal in youth, spreading to 20 feet in maturity. Handsome glossy green heart-shaped leaves. Most drought tolerant and best behaved alder. Valued in warm Southwest.	Tolerant of drought, heat, wind, and soil. Full sun, part shade.
Brachychiton populneus Bottletree	Zones 5–7, 9	Evergreen pyramidal tree to 50 feet tall. Large tapered trunk looks like a bottle. Poplarlike leaves flutter attractively in a breeze. Reddish flowers in spring. Woody seed cases in fall.	Very tolerant of drought—looks good without irrigation. Also tolerates heat, wind, and soil. Susceptible to Texas root rot.
Calocedrus decurrens Incense-cedar	Zones 1–6, 8–10	Evergreen conifer, at first slow then fast growing to 75 feet tall. Dense, pyramidal. Needs lots of room. Fragrant.	Occasional deep irrigation when young—no supplemental water for mature tree. Very tolerant of cold, heat, and soil. Resistant to oak root fungus.

Cedrus deodara (deodar cedar)

Cercidium floridum (blue palo verde)

TREES

Botanical Name Common Name	Adaptation	Description	Culture
Casuarina stricta Beefwood Mountain she oak	Zones 4–7, 9	Evergreen roundheaded tree, fast growing to 35 feet tall and 20 feet wide. Leaves are actually branchlets resembling pine needles. Useful as screen or windbreak.	Very tolerant of drought but looks better with occasional deep irrigation. Also tolerates heat, wind, soil, poor drainage, and salt air. Can be clipped into a hedge.
Catalpa speciosa Western catalpa	All zones	Deciduous, fast growing to 75 feet with spreading roundheaded habit. Dull green heart-shaped leaves. Tubular white flowers bloom in clusters above the leaves during summer.	Drought tolerant but best with occasional deep irrigation. Tolerates cold, heat, and soil. Full sun, part shade.
Cedrus species Cedar	Zones 2–10	Large evergreen conifers. *C. atlantica*, atlas cedar, to 60 feet tall. Fine-textured bluish green needles in stiff clusters. Upright branches tend to break under heavy snow. *C. deodara*, deodar cedar, fast growing to 80 feet. Light green, soft needles. Very graceful.	Drought tolerant (particularly *C. deodara*). Also tolerates cold, heat, and wind. Full sun.
Celtis species Hackberry	All zones *C. occidentalis* Zones 4–5a, 6–10 *C. australis* Zones 1–2, 8–10 *C. reticulata*	Deciduous trees related to and resembling elms but smaller and resistant to Dutch elm disease. Berries attract birds. *C. occidentalis*, common hackberry, to 50 feet tall and as wide; *C. australis*, European hackberry, to 40 feet tall and upright; *C. reticulata*, western hackberry, to 30 feet tall and upright.	Very tolerant of drought, heat, wind, and soil.
Ceratonia siliqua Carob	Zones 4–7	Evergreen dense roundheaded tree to 50 feet tall. Thick waxy dark green oval leaflets. Carob harvested from fruit on female plants.	Very tolerant of drought—looks good without irrigation. Also tolerates heat, wind, salt air, smog, and soil. Susceptible to Texas root rot.
Cercidium species Palo verde	Zones 6–10 (and inland areas of 5b)	Deciduous, fast-growing trees. *C. floridum*, blue palo verde, to 30 feet tall. Golden yellow flowers, usually the first palo verde to bloom in spring. Leaves, bark, and trunk are blue-green. *C. microphyllum*, little leaf or foothills palo verde, is smaller and less refined, to 20 feet tall. Often has multiple trunks with fine branches and yellowish green bark. Pale yellow flowers cover the tree in spring. *C. praecox*, Sonoran palo verde, to 30 feet tall. Open horizontal branching, lime green bark, and blue-green leaves. Bright yellow flowers. See also *Parkinsonia*, page 99.	Very tolerant of drought but best with occasional deep irrigation. Also tolerates heat and soil. Full sun, part shade. Resistant to Texas root rot.

Diospyros kaki (oriental persimmon)

Gleditsia triacanthos var. *inermis* (honey locust)

TREES

Botanical Name Common Name	Adaptation	Description	Culture
Chilopsis linearis Desert willow	Zones 6–9	Deciduous, fast growing to 25 feet tall and 15 feet wide. Green willowlike leaves on twisted branches. Showy white to lavender trumpet-shaped flowers in spring and summer. Nice patio tree where summer shade and winter sun are desired.	Drought tolerant but best with occasional deep irrigation. Full sun, part shade. Needs good drainage.
Cordyline australis Dracaena	Zones 4–6, 8, 10	Evergreen palmlike tree to 40 feet tall and 25 feet wide. Long narrow swordlike leaves. Best with multiple trunks. Fragrant white flowers in spring.	Very tolerant of drought—looks good without irrigation. Tolerates heat, wind, salt air, and soil. Cut back when young to encourage multiple trunks.
Cupressus species Cypress	Zones 4–10	Fast-growing evergreen conifers. *C. arizonica,* rough Arizona cypress, to 40 feet tall, grayish green foliage. Often confused with *C. glabra,* smooth Arizona cypress, to 70 feet tall. Outer bark sheds yearly revealing smooth red inner bark.	Very tolerant of drought, heat, and wind. Resistant to Texas root rot.
Diospyros kaki Oriental persimmon	Zones 3–6	Deciduous roundheaded tree to 40 feet tall and wide. Large dark green leaves turn yellow to orange to red in fall. Edible fruit in late fall or early winter. 'Fuyu' and 'Machiya' are popular cultivars.	Tolerant of drought but best with occasional deep irrigation. Also tolerates soil. Full sun, part shade. Resistant to oak root fungus.
Elaeagnus angustifolia Russian-olive	Zones 1–4, 6–10	Small deciduous tree to 20 feet tall. Silvery gray willowlike leaves. Fragrant yellow flowers in early summer are followed by yellow berries that attract birds.	Tolerant of drought, heat, cold, and wind. Resistant to Texas root rot.
Eriobotrya japonica Loquat	Zones 3–10	Evergreen dense roundheaded tree, fast growing to 30 feet tall and wide. Large, dark green coarse-looking leaves. Clusters of fragrant white flowers appear late fall to early winter. Edible fruit in summer.	Very tolerant of drought but looks better with occasional deep irrigation. Tolerates heat. Full sun, part shade.

Elaeagnus angustifolia (Russian-olive)

Grevillea robusta (silk-oak)

TREES

Botanical Name Common Name	Adaptation	Description	Culture
Eucalyptus species Eucalyptus	Zones 4–10	Many species of fast-growing evergreen trees, some too large for home gardens. Smaller scale trees include *E. ficifolia,* red-flowering gum, to 40 feet tall, large flower clusters profuse in summer and sporadically all year; *E. leucoxylon* 'Rosea', large-fruited red-flowering gum, to 25 feet tall, crimson flowers; *E. nicholii,* Nichol's willow-leaf peppermint, to 40 feet tall and weeping, crushed leaves smell like peppermint; *E. polyanthemos,* silver dollar gum, to 60 feet tall, gray-green leaves are round on young branches and lance shaped on mature branches.	Very tolerant of drought, sun, heat, and wind. Resistant to Texas root rot.
Geijera parviflora Australian willow	Zones 4–7	Evergreen, to 30 feet tall. Very graceful. Olive green willowlike leaves and slightly pendulous branches.	Tolerant of drought, heat, and wind. Full sun, good drainage. Needs little pruning.
Ginkgo biloba Maidenhair-tree Ginkgo	Zones 1–6	Deciduous, very slow growing, to 50 feet tall. May grow only 1 foot a year. Very graceful. Interesting fan-shaped leaves. Yellow fall color. 'Autumn Gold' has spectacular fall color and develops an oval crown. Plant a male tree (fruit on female trees is rank smelling).	Occasional deep irrigation until about 10 feet tall—then allow to survive on rainfall. Tolerant of heat, wind, and air pollution. Full sun. Susceptible to Texas root rot.
Gleditsia triacanthos var. *inermis* Honey locust	All zones	Deciduous, fast growing to 55 feet tall (height depends on cultivar). Delicate lacy green leaves allow filtered sunlight to pass through. Thornless cultivars include 'Sunburst', yellow new growth, and 'Ruby Lace', purplish bronze new growth.	Moderately drought tolerant. Also tolerates heat, cold, wind, and soil. Best in regions with cold winters and hot summers.
Grevillea robusta Silk-oak	Zones 4–7, 9	Evergreen pyramidal tree, fast growing to 60 feet tall. Attractive narrow dark green leaflets. Yellow-orange flowers in spring. Good large-scale specimen tree.	Very tolerant of drought—looks good without irrigation. Also tolerates heat and soil. Invasive roots—don't plant near sewer or drain lines. Can be clipped into a tall hedge.

Pinus pinea (Italian stone pine)

TREES

Botanical Name Common Name	Adaptation	Description	Culture
Hakea laurina Pincushion tree	Zones 4–7, 9	Small evergreen tree or shrub to 30 feet tall. Dense, rounded. Narrow gray-green leaves with parallel veins and red margins. Showy red pincushionlike flowers appear in late fall or winter. Good patio tree.	Very tolerant of drought, heat, wind, salt air, and soil.
Koelreuteria bipinnata Chinese flametree	Zones 4–10	Deciduous, 20 to 40 feet tall with spreading canopy. Oval leaflets remain on tree until late fall to early winter. Clusters of yellow flowers in spring are followed by rust-colored, lantern-shaped fruit.	Tolerant of drought, heat, wind, and soil.
Lagerstroemia indica Crape myrtle	Zones 3–7, 9	Deciduous small tree 10 to 30 feet tall, often multitrunked. Gray or brown and pink mottled bark. Profuse summer bloom of pink, red, purple, or white flowers crinkled like crepe paper.	Tolerates drought but best with occasional deep irrigation. Thrives in heat and full sun. 'Indian Tribes' or new hybrids are mildew resistant. All forms are resistant to Texas root rot.
Ligustrum lucidum Glossy privet	Zones 4–10	Evergreen roundheaded tree, fast growing to 35 feet tall. Glossy dark green leaves. Showy white flowers in late spring or early summer. Good shade tree.	Very tolerant of drought—looks good without irrigation. Also tolerates heat, wind, soil, and salt air. Flowers only in full sun.
Liquidambar styraciflua Sweet gum	Zones 1–6	Deciduous pyramidal tree 40 to 80 feet tall. Maplelike leaves. 'Palo Alto' has orange fall color, 'Burgundy' deep purple-red, and 'Festival' yellow, orange, and red mixture.	Drought tolerant but best with occasional deep irrigation. Soil tolerant. Full sun, part shade. Resistant to oak root fungus. Do not prune off central leader.
Maclura pomifera Osage-orange	All zones	Deciduous, fast growing to 60 feet tall. Open habit and spiny branches. Inedible 4-inch fruit resembling green oranges on female trees. Prune up for shade tree. Keep lower branches for large screen or background plant.	Tolerant of drought, heat, cold, wind, and soil. Resistant to oak root fungus.

Liquidambar styraciflua (sweet gum)

Prosopis species (mesquite)

TREES

Botanical Name Common Name	Adaptation	Description	Culture
Melaleuca species Melaleuca	Zones 4–7	Evergreen trees and shrubs, fast growing with attractive thick papery bark that peels off in layers. *M. linariifolia*, flaxleaf paperbark, to 30 feet tall, roundheaded. Gray-green leaves and white papery bark. Fluffy white flowers cover the tree spring to summer. *M. quinquenervia*, cajeput-tree, to 40 feet tall. Pale green leaves and tan papery bark. Yellowish white or lavender flowers summer and fall.	Tolerant of drought, heat, wind, salt air, and soil.
Parkinsonia aculeata Mexican palo verde Jerusalem thorn	Zones 5–9	Deciduous, fast growing to 35 feet tall with round head. Delicate, airy leaves let filtered sun through. Smooth yellowish green bark, thorny twigs. Yellow flower clusters bloom throughout spring and sporadically rest of year. See *Cercidium*, page 95, for similar trees.	Very tolerant of drought but best with occasional deep irrigation. Tolerates heat and soil. Full sun, part shade. Resistant to Texas root rot.
Pinus species Pine	All zones	Evergreen conifers suitable for large gardens. Some of the most drought tolerant include *P. eldarica*, Eldarica pine, fast growing to 80 feet tall, pyramidal; *P. pinea*, Italian stone pine, 40 to 80 feet tall, umbrellalike canopy; *P. torreyana*, Torrey pine, 40 to 60 feet tall, irregular shape; *P. sabiniana*, Digger pine, 40 to 50 feet tall, main trunk divides in two.	Check for drought-tolerant species available in your area. *P. eldarica* withstands heat, wind, and cold to 0° F. *P. pinea* and *P. torreyana* withstand inland heat and coastal conditions. *P. sabiniana* looks better with occasional water.
Pistacia chinensis Chinese pistache	Zones 3–10	Deciduous, 30 to 40 feet tall with round head. Dark green leaflets turn brilliant orange and red in fall.	Tolerant of drought, wind, and soil. Thrives in heat.
Pittosporum phillyraeoides Willow pittosporum	Zones 4–7, 9	Small tree or shrub, slow growing to 20 feet tall. Weeping form, gray-green willowlike leaves. Fragrant bell-shaped yellow flowers in early spring followed by yellow fruit.	Most drought and heat tolerant of all pittosporums. Also tolerates wind. Full sun, part shade.
Prosopis species Mesquite	Zones 7–10	Deciduous to evergreen. Size depends on amount of water received—shrubby in dry rocky soil and to 50 feet tall in deep soil where it can develop a long taproot. *P. alba*, Argentine mesquite, lacy blue-green leaves and spiny stems. *P. chilensis*, Chilean mesquite, most evergreen mesquite, fernlike foliage, dark, almost black trunk, and thorns on young trees. *P. glandulosa* var. *torreyana*, Texas native mesquite, drooping branches and lacy leaves.	Very tolerant of drought. Best with occasional water in shallow or rocky soil. Thrives in heat and sun. Resistant to Texas root rot. Some of the finest trees in the Southwest for style and shade.

Quercus agrifolia (coast live oak)   *Schinus molle* (California pepper)

TREES

Botanical Name Common Name	Adaptation	Description	Culture
Prunus cerasifera 'Atropurpurea' Purple-leaf plum	Zones 2–10	Deciduous, fast growing to 30 feet tall, roundheaded. Red-purple foliage. 1-inch white to pink flowers are showy and profuse in winter. Small edible purple plums in summer.	Very tolerant of drought and can survive on rainfall. Also tolerates heat. Needs full sun to keep foliage red-purple. Resistant to oak root fungus.
Quercus species Oak	Zones 3–6, 9–10 *Q. agrifolia* Zones 3–10 *Q. ilex* Zones 1–5a, 6–10 *Q. lobata* Zones 4–10 *Q. suber*	Excellent long-lived trees. *Q. agrifolia,* coast live oak, evergreen, to 40 feet tall and 70 feet wide, twisting gray branches. *Q. ilex,* holly oak, evergreen, to 70 feet tall and wide, dense oval canopy. *Q. lobata,* valley oak, deciduous, to 70 feet tall and wide, checkered bark and twisted branches. *Q. suber,* cork oak, evergreen, to 70 feet tall, massive trunk, and thick bark harvested for cork.	Tolerant of drought, heat, and wind. Susceptible to oak root fungus—do not apply summer water or change soil level around trunk. Holly oak and valley oak don't grow well in shade.
Rhus lancea African sumac	Zones 4–7, 9	Evergreen, to 25 feet tall and spreading wider. Graceful weeping outer branches. Glossy green leaves and attractive dark shaggy bark. Reddish berries on female trees in spring. Plant parts are poisonous.	Very tolerant of drought and heat. Full sun.
Schinus species Pepper tree	Zones 4–7, 9	*S. molle,* California pepper, evergreen, fast growing to 40 feet tall and almost as wide. Graceful weeping form, gnarled trunk, narrow green leaflets, drooping clusters of red berries fall and winter on female trees. *S. terebinthifolius,* Brazilian pepper, evergreen, to 30 feet tall, horizontal canopy, glossy dark green leaves, clusters of red berries fall and winter on female plants.	Tolerant of drought, heat, and wind. Full sun. Very susceptible to Texas root rot.
Sophora japonica Chinese scholar tree Japanese pagoda tree	All zones	Deciduous roundheaded tree to 40 feet tall and wide. Handsome dark green leaflets. Yellow fall color undependable in mild-winter areas. White flowers appear on older trees in summer.	Tolerant of drought, heat, wind, soil, and poor drainage. Full sun, part shade. Resistant to oak root fungus.
Ziziphus jujuba Chinese jujube	Zones 3–10	Deciduous, to 25 feet tall. Glossy green leaves, gnarled trunk and branches. Small yellow flowers appear followed by edible datelike fruit.	Tolerant of drought but best with occasional deep irrigation. Also tolerates heat, wind, soil, and salt air. Full sun, part shade.

Trachycarpus fortunei (windmill palm)

Washingtonia filifera (California fan palm)

PALMS

Botanical Name Common Name	Adaptation	Description	Culture
Arecastrum romanzoffianum Queen palm	Zones 5–7, 9	Showy, graceful appearance, in scale for most home landscapes. To 50 feet tall. Smooth trunk topped with feathery, shiny green fronds 10 to 15 feet long.	Occasional deep irrigation. Thrives in heat and sun. Avoid locating plants where they will be buffeted by high winds.
Brahea species Mexican blue palm Guadalupe fan palm	Zones 5–7, 9, *B. armata* Zones 5–7 *B. edulis*	Slender-trunked trees that look good alone or planted in clusters. *B. armata*, Mexican blue palm, slow growing to 40 feet tall. Silver blue fan-shaped fronds arch from the trunk to form a 12-foot canopy. Blue color most noticeable with young trees. Creamy flowers are very noticeable. *B. edulis*, Guadalupe fan palm, grows slightly faster, to 30 feet with bright light fronds forming a 10-foot crown.	Tolerant of drought, heat, sun, and wind. Best in sandy soil.
Chamaerops humilis Mediterranean fan palm	Zones 3–10	Slow growing, eventually reaching 20 feet tall and wide. May only be a 6-foot clump after 10 years. Fan-shaped leaves on dangerously spiny stems. Good as accent or barrier.	Tolerant of drought but best with occasional deep irrigation. Also tolerates heat, wind, and salt air. Full sun, part shade.
Phoenix canariensis Canary Island date palm	Zones 5–7, 9	Large-scale tree growing slowly to 60 feet tall, with dark green, shiny, feathery fronds forming a 50-foot canopy. Rough trunk covered with old leaf bases. Needs lots of space.	Very tolerant of drought, heat, wind, and salt air. Full sun.
Trachycarpus fortunei Windmill palm	Zones 3–10	Slow growing to 30 feet tall with a crown 6 to 8 feet wide. Fan-shaped leaves are dark green. Trunk is slender, covered with dark, hairy fibers. Nice compact palm for tropical effect.	Very tolerant of drought, heat, wind, and salt air. Full sun.
Washingtonia species California fan palm Mexican fan palm	Zones 4–9	*W. filifera*, California fan palm, slow growing to 60 feet tall, with a crown 15 to 20 feet wide. Fan-shaped leaves grow upward from the crown when young then droop downward. As they die they form a skirt extending part way down the trunk. *W. robusta*, Mexican fan palm, grows fast to 100 feet tall, with a crown 10 to 12 feet wide. Both are effective in clusters in large areas.	Tolerant of drought but best with some water. Tolerates heat and wind. Full sun.

Aloe species

DESERT ACCENTS

Botanical Name Common Name	Adaptation	Description	Culture
Agave americana Century plant	Zones 5-7, 9	Blue-green leaves up to 6 feet long have spines along edge and at tip. It blooms after about 10 years, producing a yellowish flower stalk 10 to 40 feet tall. The clump usually dies after flowering but suckers grow into new plants. 'Marginata' has yellow leaf margins.	Tolerant of drought. May shrivel during prolonged drought, but recovers when watered. Also tolerates heat. Full sun, part shade.
Aloe species Aloe	Zones 4-7, 9	Large group of showy succulents ranging from tiny perennials to trees. *A. arborescens,* tree aloe, grows 10 feet or taller. Spiny gray-green leaves. Red-orange flowers bloom on long, curved stems in winter. *A. barbadensis,* (also sold as *A. vera*), medicinal aloe, grows 1 to 2 feet tall. Leaves are light blue-green and upright. Striking yellow flowers appear on long stems above leaves in spring. *A. ferox,* cape aloe, usually grows to 6 feet tall. Spiny, dull green leaves are about 3 feet long and red flower spikes about 4 feet tall. *A. saponaria,* African aloe, grows to about 1 foot tall. Green leaves are tinged red in cold or in bright sun. Orange-red flowers appear atop a branched stem extending 2 feet above plant.	Very tolerant of drought, heat, and wind. Full sun, part shade. Easy to grow.
Dasylirion wheeleri Desert spoon	Zones 5-7, 9	Grows in a globe shape to 4 feet tall and slightly wider. Long, narrow gray-green leaves project from the center of the plant, making it look like a spiny sea urchin.	Occasional deep irrigation. Tolerant of exposure. Accepts some shade and reflected heat.

Echinocactus grusonii (golden barrel cactus)

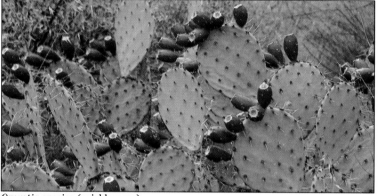

Opuntia species (prickly pear)

Yucca glauca (yucca)

DESERT ACCENTS

Botanical Name Common Name	Adaptation	Description	Culture
Echinocactus species Barrel cactus	Zones 5–7, 9	Many species of cactus identified by ribbed growth and numerous spines. *E. grusonii*, golden barrel, is one of the most popular. Grows slowly to about 4 feet tall. Prominent golden spines are attractive when backlit by the sun. Yellow flowers bloom in spring. (See *Ferocactus*, below.)	Highly tolerant of adverse conditions. Grows in intense sun and heat on available rainfall. Soil should be loose and well drained. Supplement with occasional water in driest regions for best appearance.
Ferocactus species Barrel cactus	Zones 4–10	Globe shaped when young, becoming columnar with age. Ribbed and spiny. *F. acanthodes*, compass barrel, is common in the low-desert regions. It grows slowly to 8 feet tall. Orange to yellow flowers appear in early summer. *F. wislizenii*, fishhook barrel, has distinctive, curved spines like a fishhook. Similar size and appearance as compass barrel. Red or yellow flowers appear in late summer.	See *Echinocactus*, above.
Fouquieria splendens Ocotillo	Zones 6–10	Long thin branches up to 15 feet long sprout fountainlike from the ground. Small leaves emerge to cover thorny branches when water is abundant, will drop off during dry periods. Bright orange-red flowers appear in clusters at branch tips in spring.	Very drought tolerant and will not accept overwatering. Needs full sun and good drainage.
Hesperaloe parviflora Hesperaloe	Zones 5–10	To 4 feet tall with long, narrow, dark green, swordlike leaves. White fibers curl from leaf edges. Red to pink flowers on tall arching stalks bloom above foliage for several months in summer.	Looks good without irrigation. Tolerates reflected heat. Full sun.

Center right: *Agave americana* (century plant)
Left foreground and background: *Aloe* species

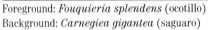

Foreground: *Fouquieria splendens* (ocotillo)
Background: *Carnegiea gigantea* (saguaro)

Center right: *Dasylirion wheeleri* (desert spoon)

Opuntia species (cholla)

DESERT ACCENTS

Botanical Name Common Name	Adaptation	Description	Culture
Opuntia species Prickly pear Cholla	Zones vary, depending on species	Many species, some of which are cold hardy. Two basic forms are prickly pears and chollas. Prickly pears consist of segments or pads that are typically flat and oval in shape. The chollas are woody, upright, and often covered with sharp thorns. Some of the best species include *O. bigelovii*, teddybear cactus, an upright, cholla-type with yellowish spines. *O. ficus-indica*, spineless prickly pear, has flat, smooth pads or segments that connect to grow to 10 feet or more. *O. microdasys*, bunny ears, has bright green segments with contrasting tufts of tiny golden bristles. There are dozens of other species, some of which grow in winter-snow areas. Check local sources.	Survives on rainfall in most regions, but looks better with supplemental irrigation during dry periods. Accepts range of exposures. Provide with loose, well-drained soil.
Yucca species Yucca	Zones vary, depending on species	Includes many different kinds of plants from low-growing perennials to trees. Here are a few that make good accents in the landscape. *Y. aloifolia*, Spanish-bayonet, to 10 feet or taller. Dark green, sharp-pointed leaves reach over 2 feet long. White flowers bloom in clusters above foliage in summer. *Y. gloriosa*, soft-tip yucca, grows as a multitrunked tree to 15 feet tall. It resembles Spanish-bayonet except that leaf tips aren't sharp. *Y. elata*, soaptree yucca, can grow to 15 feet tall, but is usually smaller. Narrow gray-green leaves up to 4 feet long hang down around the trunk when they die. White flower clusters are borne on tall stalks above leaves in late spring. *Y. recurvifolia*, grows 6 to 10 feet tall. Leaves are blue-green, strap shaped, and up to 3 feet long. Leaves curve out from plant then down toward ground. Clusters of white flowers bloom on stalks above the leaves in early summer.	Very tolerant of drought and heat. Full sun. Good accents around pools.

	Total Inches Rain	Inches July/August	Last Spring Frost	First Fall Frost	Number of 90° + F Days in July	Growing Season (days)	January	February	March	April	May	June	July	August	September	October	November	December
ARIZONA																		
Casa Grande	8.1	2.5	3/9	11/19	31	255	61/35	72/33	72/37	87/46	89/51	105/66	106/77	105/76	99/69	90/58	77/42	74/42
Douglas	16	7.4	4/8	11/6	23	212	57/32	68/32	65/34	77/45	85/49	93/61	91/66	94/64	89/57	78/47	71/35	67/30
Flagstaff	19.3	5.1	6/3	9/29	1	118	41/14	44/17	48/20	57/27	67/33	76/40	81/50	78/49	74/41	63/31	51/22	43/16
Globe	13	3.8	3/9	11/13	27	229	55/32	65/35	62/34	76/45	80/46	94/60	94/68	95/68	88/63	80/51	68/40	61/36
Nogales	24	9.8	3/30	11/14	22	229	61/31	71/28	68/30	79/39	82/43	95/55	91/65	91/64	89/58	81/49	74/34	69/32
Phoenix	7	2	2/5	12/6	31	304	65/38	69/41	74/45	84/52	93/60	101/68	105/77	102/76	98/69	88/57	75/45	66/38
Sedona	16.7	3.8	n/a	n/a	26	365	52/28	63/30	62/29	77/38	78/44	95/55	98/63	96/63	89/57	79/48	64/36	60/32
Tucson	11	4.7	3/19	11/19	29	245	63/38	67/40	71/44	81/50	90/57	98/66	98/74	95/72	93/67	84/56	72/45	65/39
Winslow	7.3	2.7	5/2	10/17	26	168	46/20	53/25	60/29	70/37	80/45	90/54	94/63	91/61	85/53	73/41	58/28	47/21
Yuma	2.7	.62	1/12	12/26	31	348	67/43	73/46	78/50	86/57	93/64	101/71	106/81	104/81	100/74	90/82	76/50	68/44
CALIFORNIA																		
Bakersfield	5.7	.03	2/21	11/25	29	277	57/37	63/41	69/44	75/50	84/56	91/62	99/69	96/67	91/62	80/53	68/44	57/38
Fresno	10.2	.02	2/9	12/1	29	295	55/36	61/39	67/41	74/46	83/52	90/57	98/63	96/61	91/56	80/49	66/41	55/37
Lancaster	9.6	1	3/31	10/31	27	215	54/31	61/32	69/33	76/45	69/48	90/63	96/67	94/66	86/58	81/49	69/35	62/38
Los Angeles	14	.04	1/3	12/28	4	359	66/47	68/48	69/50	70/53	73/56	76/59	83/63	84/64	82/63	78/59	73/52	68/48
Oakland	19	.1	1/11	12/28	2	351	57/42	62/47	62/46	67/50	64/52	68/56	72/57	73/60	72/59	70/55	64/49	59/49
Palm Springs	5.3	.48	1/18	12/18	31	334	70/42	83/47	77/44	91/55	87/56	106/69	110/75	106/75	100/67	93/61	82/48	72/47
Pasadena	18.9	.07	2/3	12/13	0	313	67/45	76/48	68/43	75/50	71/50	82/57	85/60	88/63	84/59	82/56	79/51	69/50
Red Bluff	22	.22	3/6	12/5	28	274	54/37	59/40	64/42	72/47	81/54	89/62	98/64	96/64	91/60	78/52	64/43	55/38
Riverside	10.2	0	3/6	11/26	30	265	65/42	76/44	67/42	78/48	72/51	88/57	96/60	92/63	87/57	84/53	79/45	69/47
Sacramento	17.2	.06	2/6	12/10	23	307	53/37	59/40	64/42	71/45	79/50	86/55	93/57	91/57	88/53	77/49	64/42	53/38
San Bernar.	16.1	.14	3/15	11/23	30	253	68/42	78/44	68/41	80/49	71/50	91/58	99/62	96/64	90/58	87/54	81/47	70/46
San Diego	9.4	.08	n/a	n/a	0	365	65/46	66/48	68/50	68/54	69/57	71/60	75/64	77/65	76/63	74/58	70/51	66/47
San Frans.	20.6	.06	1/7	12/29	0	356	56/46	59/48	60/48	61/49	62/51	64/53	64/53	65/54	69/55	68/55	63/51	57/47
San Jose	13.6	.09	2/10	12/6	3	299	57/38	65/44	63/42	73/47	68/48	79/56	82/56	80/58	79/55	74/51	66/45	60/46
San Luis Ob.	21.9	.05	1/30	12/16	5	320	64/44	71/47	64/42	70/44	65/47	73/52	79/53	79/56	77/52	75/49	70/49	67/49
Santa Ana	12.9	.06	2/7	12/7	0	303	70/47	75/47	68/45	74/53	74/54	77/60	84/61	83/65	82/62	79/59	79/50	70/52
Santa Barb.	17.4	.04	1/22	12/19	0	331	66/42	71/44	66/44	70/49	69/52	71/55	75/57	77/61	76/58	74/55	76/47	68/51
COLORADO																		
Alamosa	7	2.3	6/8	9/12	1	96	35/-7	40/5	47/15	58/24	68/33	78/41	82/48	80/46	74/36	63/25	48/12	37/60
Boulder	19	3.4	5/3	10/11	0	161	41/16	44/19	48/23	59/33	68/43	78/51	84/57	82/56	75/47	64/37	50/25	43/19
Denver	15.5	3.1	4/26	10/14	15	171	44/14	52/24	54/26	63/39	75/46	86/57	88/61	83/57	81/49	69/37	51/20	49/21
Durango	18.5	4.2	5/28	9/26	10	121	36/4	50/17	51/19	66/31	70/35	86/46	86/53	86/52	80/45	69/30	54/23	45/18
Ft. Collins	15	2.9	5/7	9/29	12	145	40/10	51/22	53/24	63/36	73/46	79/45	86/59	80/56	80/49	67/37	52/25	47/21
Grand Junction	8.4	1.5	4/16	10/24	26	191	37/16	44/23	53/30	65/39	76/48	86/57	93/64	89/62	81/53	68/42	51/29	39/20
Greely	12.2	2.4	5/5	9/30	22	148	41/10	53/22	57/23	66/37	77/47	90/56	91/59	85/56	85/48	72/35	54/24	47/19
La Junta	14	8.3	4/28	10/9	21	164	44/11	56/22	61/27	73/42	83/54	93/62	94/64	88/61	87/52	72/36	58/22	50/16
Pueblo	11.9	3.8	4/23	10/14	22	174	43/12	57/19	60/24	70/39	81/49	91/57	94/61	88/60	86/49	72/35	59/23	52/19
Sterling	15	4	5/7	9/30	0	146	36/6	51/21	51/24	65/38	76/49	89/59	92/62	85/59	83/50	69/34	50/24	43/16
IDAHO																		
Boise	11.5	.4	4/23	10/17	19	177	36/21	44/27	52/30	61/36	71/44	78/51	90/58	88/57	78/48	65/39	49/31	39/25
Burley	9.7	.8	5/16	9/23	5	130	32/13	47/19	47/25	67/34	62/40	82/53	84/54	84/53	74/43	67/32	48/26	41/27
Caldwell	10.8	.5	5/7	10/3	20	149	27/14	44/24	55/30	74/41	69/43	89/58	91/58	91/58	79/47	67/36	50/29	44/31
Cr. D'Alene	26	1.7	5/8	10/6	6	151	35/20	46/27	47/30	67/35	65/42	80/51	82/53	88/54	69/45	60/37	43/29	37/25
Idaho Falls	8.9	1	5/15	9/19	8	127	19/0	30/7	42/21	64/31	61/38	82/50	85/52	83/48	73/41	63/30	43/22	34/20
Moscow	9.7	1.6	5/6	10/6	4	153	31/14	48/19	48/25	66/34	61/39	81/52	83/53	83/52	74/41	66/33	48/26	42/27
Pocatello	22.6	1.2	4/28	10/6	5	161	32/18	46/29	45/30	64/36	62/38	81/48	82/49	86/51	66/43	59/35	42/28	37/26
Twin Falls	10.8	1	5/18	9/26	16	131	32/14	39/20	46/25	58/33	68/41	76/47	89/54	86/52	76/43	63/34	46/25	35/15

	Total Inches Rain	Inches July/August	Last Spring Frost	First Fall Frost	Number of 90°+F Days in July	Growing Season (days)	January	February	March	April	May	June	July	August	September	October	November	December
MONTANA																		
Billings	14.1	1.9	5/15	9/25	12	133	31/12	37/18	42/23	56/33	66/43	74/51	86/58	84/56	71/46	61/37	45/26	36/18
Glasgow	10.9	2.9	5/19	9/19	9	123	19/-5	25/5	36/15	55/31	67/42	74/50	84/57	83/55	70/44	59/34	39/19	26/7
Great Falls	15	2.3	5/9	9/25	9	139	29/12	36/17	40/21	54/32	65/41	72/49	84/55	82/53	70/48	59/37	43/26	35/18
Helena	11.4	1.9	5/2	10/2	7	153	28/7	36/15	42/19	55/30	65/39	72/47	84/52	82/50	70/41	59/32	43/21	33/13
Missoula	13.3	1.8	5/18	9/23	10	128	29/13	36/19	44/23	57/31	66/38	72/45	84/49	83/47	71/40	57/31	41/24	32/17
NEVADA																		
Carson	11.5	.4	5/25	9/19	23	117	45/19	57/20	52/24	70/33	62/35	87/51	91/49	91/51	80/41	70/31	61/27	52/27
Elko	9.8	1	6/1	9/12	20	103	36/10	42/17	48/21	59/28	68/35	77/42	90/49	88/46	79/36	66/28	49/21	38/13
Ely	8.7	1.2	5/26	9/22	9	119	38/9	41/14	47/19	56/26	66/34	76/40	86/48	84/47	76/37	64/28	49/19	40/12
Hawthorne	5.9	.8	5/1	10/16	25	168	44/20	56/25	55/27	71/39	66/41	89/59	94/58	91/58	83/48	73/40	61/31	55/28
Las Vegas	3.8	.9	3/16	11/10	31	239	56/33	61/37	68/42	77/50	87/59	97/67	101/75	101/73	95/65	81/53	66/41	57/34
Reno	7.2	.5	5/8	10/10	22	155	45/18	51/23	56/25	64/30	72/37	80/42	91/47	89/45	82/39	70/30	56/24	46/20
Tonopah	4.2	.8	5/16	10/12	25	149	43/17	56/24	50/21	68/34	63/37	86/54	91/56	88/56	79/46	72/38	58/26	50/25
Winnemucca	8.5	.5	5/11	9/29	23	141	41/16	47/21	52/23	61/29	70/37	79/44	91/51	89/47	80/38	67/29	52/22	43/18
NEW MEXICO																		
Alamogordo	10.2	3.8	4/6	11/5	30	213	57/28	63/30	67/34	77/44	85/54	97/63	96/64	97/66	92/60	80/49	70/37	63/32
Albuquerque	7.8	2.7	4/13	10/28	23	198	47/23	53/27	59/32	70/41	80/51	89/60	92/65	90/63	83/57	72/45	57/32	47/25
Carlsbad	10.8	2.4	3/29	11/4	29	220	52/26	64/32	69/35	79/48	89/59	97/65	97/69	99/71	95/65	77/51	71/37	66/34
Deming	6.8	3	4/2	11/1	27	213	54/28	64/29	64/32	73/42	80/46	93/60	94/65	96/67	90/59	77/47	69/34	61/30
Gallup	9.1	3.6	5/5	10/9	7	157	39/9	50/16	52/19	65/28	71/36	85/48	85/57	85/56	78/49	70/35	56/25	51/23
Hobbs	14.4	4	4/10	11/3	30	207	54/24	65/34	69/36	76/46	86/58	94/64	93/65	95/67	92/62	78/50	70/37	65/33
Roswell	10.6	3.1	4/7	10/31	30	207	52/25	63/33	68/36	77/48	87/59	96/67	97/71	95/71	92/65	77/51	69/37	63/31
Santa Fe	13.2	6.3	4/24	10/19	3	178	36/15	46/22	49/25	61/36	71/43	85/54	85/57	84/58	78/49	69/40	55/30	47/17
Socorro	7.9	2.9	4/5	10/22	24	196	49/19	60/24	63/27	74/37	81/42	92/54	92/60	91/61	86/55	76/39	66/27	59/25
OREGON																		
Baker	12.7	2.7	5/12	10/3	9	144	28/11	48/23	48/25	68/30	62/36	82/47	84/46	86/49	72/40	63/32	46/25	40/26
Bend	12	.8	6/8	9/7	1	91	42/17	53/23	50/23	65/28	58/32	78/43	80/43	84/48	69/36	63/31	48/24	43/26
Klamath Falls	14	.7	5/18	9/26	8	131	32/11	49/24	47/25	64/32	58/34	81/50	84/50	86/54	71/44	63/36	47/28	42/26
Medford	12	.6	5/6	10/14	15	161	39/25	46/31	53/34	62/40	70/46	78/53	88/59	85/57	78/51	63/42	49/34	42/30
Salem	21	.6	4/1	10/31	18	213	44/29	52/31	57/33	64/37	72/43	79/49	89/54	88/53	82/47	67/39	53/34	44/31
UTAH																		
Beaver	11.3	2.4	6/6	9/18	12	104	42/12	51/16	51/19	65/30	65/37	86/46	87/52	86/51	78/44	69/34	56/24	50/20
Cedar City	10.3	2.2	5/9	10/6	19	150	45/18	54/21	51/23	68/35	67/41	87/54	89/59	89/58	80/49	72/37	58/27	52/27
Ogden	16.2	1.3	5/6	10/8	18	155	36/18	47/25	48/28	68/42	65/43	88/60	91/62	86/59	78/51	68/41	51/31	43/28
S.L. City	15.2	1.6	4/13	10/22	25	192	37/18	43/23	51/28	62/37	72/44	81/51	91/60	90/59	80/49	66/38	50/28	39/21
Spanish Fork	18	1.6	4/28	10/13	24	168	36/17	45/21	49/25	68/37	67/41	89/55	92/60	89/58	81/50	70/42	53/32	45/28
Vernal	7.8	1.1	5/26	9/21	15	118	35/12	46/18	48/19	67/34	69/38	90/50	89/53	86/53	79/44	65/33	48/21	40/17
WASHINGTON																		
Spokane	17.4	1	4/12	10/13	10	184	31/20	39/25	46/29	57/35	66/43	74/49	84/55	82/54	72/47	58/37	42/29	34/24
Walla Walla	16	.8	3/31	6/5	15	219	39/27	47/33	54/37	63/43	71/50	79/56	89/62	86/61	77/54	64/45	49/36	42/31
Wenatchee	9.4	.6	4/24	10/14	12	173	31/19	49/29	56/32	71/39	69/44	85/56	86/57	91/58	72/46	64/35	51/30	38/25
Yakima	8	.4	5/15	10/22	14	190	36/19	46/25	55/29	64/35	73/43	79/49	88/53	86/51	78/44	65/35	48/28	39/23
WYOMING																		
Casper	11.2	1.5	5/19	9/29	11	133	34/13	38/16	43/19	55/30	61/39	76/47	87/55	86/53	74/43	61/34	45/23	36/16
Cheyenne	14.6	3.3	5/14	10/2	6	141	38/15	41/17	43/20	55/30	65/40	78/48	84/54	82/53	73/43	62/34	47/23	40/18
Jackson	15.2	1.9	6/20	8/31	0	72	28/2	37/5	41/14	61/20	59/32	79/40	78/40	78/39	71/32	61/21	41/19	33/17
Laramie	10.1	2.5	5/29	9/19	0	113	33/6	40/9	40/13	53/26	64/33	80/46	81/49	76/46	72/39	60/28	44/18	38/16
Rawlins	9.8	3.1	6/1	9/21	0	112	30/9	41/15	38/17	57/30	64/36	82/49	82/53	77/50	72/41	59/32	42/21	35/20
Rock Springs	8.8	1.2	6/3	9/11	6	100	34/11	44/17	39/16	60/31	64/35	84/50	84/52	79/49	74/39	62/31	43/21	36/19

Catalog Sources of Seeds, Plants, and Gardening Equipment

The best places to buy plants and gardening equipment are your local nursery and garden stores, where you can examine what you are buying and don't have to pay shipping charges. But, if your local nursery or garden store can't get what you need, you may want to contact one of the following. This list is by no means complete, but it will give you a place to start. Catalog policies vary; contact each company for current policy and prices.

Bernardo Beach Native Plant Farm
Star Route 7, Box 145
Veguita, NM 87062
Southwestern trees, shrubs, and wildflowers. Plants only.

Blue Oak Nursery
2731 Mountain Oak Lane
Rescue, CA 95672
California trees, shrubs, and wildflowers. Plants only.

Cornflower Farms
Box 896
Elkgrove, CA 95624
California native plants.

Dry Country Plants
3904 Highway 70 East
Las Cruces, NM 88001
Southern New Mexico native plants; specializes in flowering perennials.

Horizon Seeds, Inc.
Box 886, East Highway 60
Hereford, TX 79045
Native prairie grasses. Seeds only.

New Mexico Cactus Research
Box 787, Dept. 102
Belon, NM 87002
Cactus and succulents. Seeds only.

The Theodore Payne Foundation
10459 Tuxford Street
Sun Valley, CA 91352
California trees, shrubs, and wildflowers. Seeds and plants.

Plants of the Southwest
1812 Second Street
Santa Fe, NM 87501
Southwestern trees, shrubs, and wildflowers. Seeds and plants.

The Shop in the Sierra
Box 1
Midpines, CA 95345
California trees, shrubs, and wildflowers. Plants only.

Southwestern Native Seeds
Box 50503
Tucson, AZ 85703
Native plants of the western United States and Mexico. Seeds only.

Submatic
Box 246
Lubbock, TX 79408
Drip irrigation equipment and supplies.

The Urban Farmer
2833 Vicente Street
San Francisco, CA 94116
Gardening equipment, including drip irrigation supplies.

Wildflower Seed Company
Box 406
St. Helena, CA 94574
Variety of wildflower mixes for each region of the United States.

For more information on xeriscaping, contact your local water district office or write to:
National Xeriscape Council, Inc.
940 East 51st Street
Austin, TX 78751

U.S. Measure and Metric Measure Conversion Chart

	Symbol	When you know:	Multiply by:	To find:	Rounded Measures for Quick Reference		
Mass (Weight)	oz	ounces	28.35	grams	1 oz		= 30 g
	lb	pounds	0.45	kilograms	4 oz		= 115 g
	g	grams	0.035	ounces	8 oz		= 225 g
	kg	kilograms	2.2	pounds	16 oz	= 1 lb	= 450 g
					32 oz	= 2 lb	= 900 g
					36 oz	= 2¼ lb	= 1000g (1 kg)
Volume	pt	pints	0.47	liters	1 c	= 8 oz	= 250 ml
	qt	quarts	0.95	liters	2 c (1 pt)	= 16 oz	= 500 ml
	gal	gallons	3.785	liters	4 c (1 qt)	= 32 oz	= 1 liter
	ml	milliliters	0.034	fluid ounces	4 qt (1 gal)	= 128 oz	= 3¾ liter
Length	in.	inches	2.54	centimeters	⅜ in.		= 1 cm
	ft	feet	30.48	centimeters	1 in.		= 2.5 cm
	yd	yards	0.9144	meters	2 in.		= 5 cm
	mi	miles	1.609	kilometers	2½ in.		= 6.5 cm
	km	kilometers	0.621	miles	12 in. (1 ft)		= 30 cm
	m	meters	1.094	yards	1 yd		= 90 cm
	cm	centimeters	0.39	inches	100 ft		= 30 m
					1 mi		= 1.6 km
Temperature	°F	Fahrenheit	5/9 (after subtracting 32)	Celsius	32°F		= 0°C
	°C	Celsius	9/5 (then add 32)	Fahrenheit	212°F		= 100°C
Area	in.²	square inches	6.452	square centimeters	1 in.²		= 6.5 cm²
	ft²	square feet	929.0	square centimeters	1 ft²		= 930 cm²
	yd²	square yards	8361.0	square centimeters	1 yd²		= 8360 cm²
	a.	acres	0.4047	hectares	1 a.		= 4050 m²

INDEX

*Note: Boldface type indicates
principal references; italic
type indicates illustrations.*